Foreign Ownership
of U.S. Farmland

Foreign Ownership of U.S. Farmland

An Economic Analysis of Regulation

David N. Laband
University of Maryland
Baltimore County

LexingtonBooks
D.C. Heath and Company
Lexington, Massachusetts
Toronto

Library of Congress Cataloging in Publication Data

Laband, David N.
   Foreign ownership of U.S. farmland.

   Bibliography: p.
   Includes index.
   1. Farms—United States—Foreign ownership. I. Title.
HD256.L33   1984   333.33′5   83–48639
ISBN 0–669–07305–9

Published simultaneously in Canada

Printed in the United States of America

International Standard Book Number: 0–669–07305–9

Library of Congress Catalog Card Number: 83–48639

To the Memory of My Father

Contents

Figures and Tables

Preface and
Acknowledgments

Instead of being viewed as a rival, foreign investment ought to be considered a most valued auxiliary, conducing to put in motion a greater portion of useful enterprise, and a greater quantity of productive labor, than could exist without it. —*Alexander Hamilton* (1791)

The history of U.S. economic development begins with the letter *F*, for *foreign investment*. Foreign investment has played a major, if not preeminent role in economic development in the United States. Virtually all investment undertaken in colonial times was underwritten by European capital. Throughout the ensuing years and until the recent past, foreign investors in the United States have been generally tolerated and in many instances encouraged by the various states.

In the latter half of the 1970s, foreign investment in the United States came under increasing public scrutiny at the same time as it was becoming a burning political issue; it remains so in 1983. Farmers are up in arms across the land over what they feel is overparticipation in the domestic land market by foreigners. The fear is voiced that rich foreigners, for a variety of reasons, are very willing to buy farmland at premium prices, endangering the so-called family farm as an economic institution. Numerous states passed legislation in the 1970s that partially or totally restricted nonresident aliens (NRAs) from owning farmland. Farm lobby groups were, without exception, the driving force behind the push for regulation.

One has to take only a cursory look at the market for U.S. farmland to discover a number of interesting and highly relevant facts relating to foreign participation in it. First, the incidence of foreign ownership of domestic farmland is microscopically small. On June 20, 1978, the Director of Economics at the U.S. Department of Agriculture (USDA) testified before the subcommittee on Family Farms, Rural Development, and Special Studies of the House Committee on Agriculture, concluding that at most, 1 percent of the privately owned land in the United States is held by foreigners. Even if all of that were farmland (which it is not) it would be only slightly more than 1 percent of all U.S. farmland. In terms of turnover, roughly 3 percent of domestic farmland changes hands in any one year, and of that only a scant 2.25 percent is bought by outsiders. At the current rate of foreign investment it would take about nineteen years for foreigners to acquire ownership of an additional 1 percent of U.S. farmland, provided they did not sell or otherwise transfer the land back to U.S. citizens.

Second, though prices per acre of U.S. farmland rose dramatically over the 1960–80 period, the overwhelming majority of the increase can be attributed to increases in prices paid for farm crops, and, especially, to bidding among established farmers. Statistics prepared by the USDA indicate that in 1976, for example, 65 percent of the land that changed hands went to active farmers for expansion of their current farming operations. Other farmland skyrocketed in value as the so-called urban fringe was expanded ever outward. Though it is true that foreigners have been known to pay above-market prices for certain farmland investments, other sales have occurred at below average-market value.

Third, the land is not being gobbled up by wealthy Arab sheiks who are anxious to cash in newly acquired petrodollars for a more viable portfolio holding. The majority of farmland purchases over the period in question have been made by Canadians and western Europeans, especially the British. Fears that undesirable outsiders might gain unwanted control or influence in the U.S. agricultural system seem to be generally groundless.

Fourth, a variety of powerful interests have ranged themselves in opposition to legislative restrictions on foreign ownership of U.S. real estate, including real estate agents, businessmen, and even some farmers. In spite of this opposition, twenty-five states have passed laws that restrict, in some fashion, the ownership rights of foreigners to private farmland, and similar legislation has been proposed in a number of additional states.

This book provides an in-depth analysis of foreign participation in the market for U.S. farmland. Chapters 1 and 2 highlight the history of land-ownership in the United States, the history of regulation against foreigners, motives for foreign investment in U.S. real estate, and recent trends in land-ownership. This provides a necessary perspective for further discussion of the problem of foreign investment in U.S. farmland.

The conventional economic implications of foreign investment for members of the farming community are examined in chapter 3. The conclusion reached is inevitable: foreign investment in U.S. farmland is so minute that it constitutes no threat to farmers as a whole, or to any subgroup thereof. Restriction of entry into the domestic farmland market is not only unwarranted, but it may induce other countries to impose similar restrictions against U.S. investment abroad.

We are left, seemingly, on the horns of a dilemma. If foreign participation in the domestic farmland market poses no threat to farmers, how can we explain the fact that farmers in so many states have lobbied to obtain statutory limitations on foreign investment? Are farmers acting irrationally—wasting economic resources in political influence-buying that has no payoff?

It seem premature, at best, to label any behavior as irrational based on standards imposed by the external observer. It is much more useful, not to mention empirically correct, to assume that the behavior is rational, and find an explanation for it. It is in this vein that chapters 4 and 5 are written.

Chapter 4 presents an economic theory that argues that family farmers find it in their economic best interest to regulate the market in U.S. farmland. Chapter 5 seeks to explain the prevailing pattern of legal restrictions as resulting from the relative political strength of small, family farmers in each state.

Having resolved the dilemma before us, we turn our attention to the legal status of foreign investment in agricultural land in chapter 6. A state-by-state survey of legal provisions affecting foreign investment is presented, as well as a brief look at states that have tried—but failed—to enact legal restrictions against nonresident alien ownership of farmland.

Chapter 7 deals with two related topics—restriction of corporate farming, and nationalism as rent-seeking behavior analogous to that discussed in chapters 4 and 5. The final chapter reviews the basic conclusions and underscores the potentially fruitful combination of public-choice economics and other aspects of agricultural economics, as well as the other social sciences.

A particular debt of gratitude is owed to the members of the Center for Study of Public Choice, especially to James M. Buchanan and Robert D. Tollison. Their encouragement of individual intellectual creativity has marked me in ways that extend far beyond the scope of this book. Additional support and encouragement was received from Robert E. McCormick, Richard Kirk, J. Paxton Marshall, and, more than she realizes, Mrs. Betty T. Ross. Assistance from Mr. J. Peter DeBraal and Dale Schian of the USDA is gratefully acknowledged. John Sophocleus undertook the tedious task of reading the entire manuscript with a critical eye. For that service and many others, my debt in his direction is substantial. Last on paper, but first in spirit—thanks to my lovely wife, Anne.

1 Foreign Direct Investment in U.S. Farmland

From the outset it will be necessary to distinguish between farmland and other types of real estate. In general, real estate is taken to encompass urban as well as rural land, developed or undeveloped. Apartment buildings, residential districts, and factories constitute real estate. Farmland, as a specific class of real estate, is usually classified as rural acreage devoted to agricultural production.

A Brief History of Foreign Investment in the United States

Foreign investment during Alexander Hamilton's day was welcomed in the American colonies. Virtually all investment in the earliest colonial settlements was based on foreign capital. An English joint stock company was responsible for outfitting the colonists who came to Jamestown in 1607.[1] During this colonial period, British, Dutch, and French investments on the North American continent were largely responsible for erecting the economic infrastructure that stimulated the country's subsequent economic development. An *alien* owner was, by definition, someone who was not a British subject. An individual could not hold legal title to land unless he was recognized as a citizen by the British crown. The ultimate method of obtaining the right to own property was naturalization, which was difficult to obtain since it required passage of a private act by the local legislative body.[2]

Toward the onset of the Revolutionary War the period of extensive British investment in the American colonies came to a close as many investors liquidated their holdings. Security of tenure in these particular property rights had become much less certain, driving British citizens to invest elsewhere. After the success of the Revolution was established and the Constitution for the new nation adopted, British investors, among others, turned once more to the new world as a repository for their investment capital.

The question of how to handle foreign ownership of land and other assets in the newly formed United States was left up to the states to decide individually. Foreign ownership of land was generally permitted, provided the land was purchased and not inherited. When difficulties previous to the Revolution were removed, speculation in U.S. land picked up in the late 1700s and continued, with ebbs and flows, for the next century. Land of-

1

fices run by private land investment companies sprang up all over Europe, extolling the virtues of the new nation. Immigration, particularly by Europeans, was actively encouraged by the states. Around the turn of the nineteenth century, hundreds of thousands of acres of U.S. land were purchased by groups of European investors who, correctly, anticipated a rise in land prices with the coming western expansion. During the 1790s, for example, the Holland Land Company purchased 3.5 million acres of land in New York, about one-seventh of the state's area, and resold it to incoming settlers at a 5- to 6-percent rate of return.[3]

Thus, land policy with respect to foreigners had undergone a complete about-face by the nineteenth century, from the presumption that alien (non-British) ownership of U.S. land was prohibited unless permitted by statute, to the presumption that alien (non-American) ownership was permitted unless restricted by the states. Over time the proportion of foreign investment to domestic investment declined as productivity and development proceeded in the growing country. Nevertheless, the flow of capital from foreign countries into the United States during the nineteenth century continued to rise in absolute terms (see table 1–1).

Table 1–1 shows that from 1790 to 1820 the flow of foreign capital into the United States was relatively stable. The significant increase that began in the antebellum 1830s corresponds to the rapid rise in the building of this country's network of highways and canals, as well as one of the upswings in speculative fever, of which there were several waves in the 1800s. The level of capital inflow declined as many of these ventures proved less profitable than expected, only to be stimulated again the 1850s by the westward expan-

Table 1–1
Foreign Investment in the United States, 1790–1900
(millions of dollars)

Year	Net Liability
1790	61
1800	83
1810	85
1820	88
1830	75
1840	261
1850	217
1860	377
1870	1,252
1880	1,584
1890	2,894
1900	2,501

Source: *Historical Statistics of the United States,* Department of Commerce, Bureau of the Census (Washington, D.C.: Government Printing Office, 1960), p. 566.

sion of the railroads. The postbellum era was characterized by a doubling of foreign investment every five years, followed by a sharp decline in the late 1870s as a result of a crash in the land speculation market, and then a steady rise to the end of the century.[4]

The early to mid-1800s witnessed wave after wave of speculative fever that centered on the farm and ranch lands of the midwestern and western states. Land companies, territories, and states were involved heavily in trying to attract not only easterners, but foreigners as well to the developing lands in the interior of the country. Official efforts to promote emigration to the Dakota territory, Kansas, Nebraska, and Minnesota developed as early as 1855 by government-sponsored companies. In 1864 the Minnesota state legislature authorized the Secretary of State to do *everything* that might enhance and encourage immigration to the state.[5] Promotional pamphlets were published and distributed to prospective settlers in the United States and abroad. In addition to those written in English, many of the pamphlets were made available in Swedish, Norwegian, German, and Dutch translations.

A high percentage of the companies in the vanguard of promoting immigration were composed of foreign investors. They were attracted to speculative ventures in U.S. farmland as success story upon success story raised expectations of the profitability of investing in the United States. One potential English investor who was in Kentucky in 1795 looking for promising land deals commented on the 100-percent rise in land values in the previous ten years, and added that in many instances values had risen from 300 to 500 percent. Significant investments were also made by individuals: France's Joseph Picquet bought over eleven thousand acres of Illinois farmland and England's C.A. Murray bought twenty thousand acres in Wisconsin. British capitalists bought up numerous cattle companies and vast holdings of farmland in the Midwest.[6]

In the latter half of the nineteenth century one of the primary sources of land acquisition for foreigners was the railroads. Land-grant railroads raised substantial sums of money by selling off hundreds of thousands of acres granted them by the federal government. Much of this land was purchased by foreigners. Five hundred thousand acres were purchased by English investors in 1857 from the Dubuque and Pacific Railroad, and another forty thousand acres sold by the Sioux City and St. Paul Railroad in the 1880s went to a London-based land company.[7] Additional land was available to foreigners as incentive for investing in the railroads' stocks and bonds, and as payment for default on some of these notes. Defaults by states on their bonds, which were paid off with state land, mortgage companies owned by foreigners, and cattle ranches were additional avenues that enabled foreigners to add to their holdings of U.S. farmland until the twentieth century.

The 1890s and early 1900s were the high points of foreign investment in U.S. lands. Prior to World War I foreign-owned, but U.S.–based land companies owned between 30 and 35 million acres in the United States. As table 1-1 shows, this was a period of tremendous increases in foreign investment in the United States. The possibility of increasing foreign control over U.S. assets finally stimulated public concern around the turn of the twentieth century, and it was at this time that the first restrictions of foreign ownership of U.S. land emerged.

The History of State Regulation

The first restrictive legislation aimed at foreign, and especially at nonresident, landowners appeared in the midwestern states. The opposition against foreigners was supported by the Granger movement, and became such a burning political issue that it was one of the planks in the Populist platform of 1892.[8] The issue was brought to the forefront, several sources said, by accounts of William Scully, an Irishman who accumulated vast amounts of farmland in several midwestern states. In the four states of Illinois, Missouri, Kansas, and Nebraska, Scully had amassed an empire of land amounting to 220,000 acres at a cost to him of $1,350,000.[9]

The first state law that prohibited nonresident aliens from acquiring real estate was signed by the governor of Illinois in 1887. Colorado, Minnesota, Nebraska, and Wisconsin followed suit in that same year. Iowa joined them in 1888, as did Idaho (1891), and Missouri (1895). In all, thirteen states passed legislation that sharply restricted or banned outright any further acquisition of U.S. lands by foreigners.

As populism died out toward the turn of the twentieth century, opposition to the foreign presence in the U.S. land market faded, a result, perhaps, of generally favorable conditions in the agricultural sector. A second round of restrictive legislation began in California in 1920, aimed at prohibiting landownership by the Japanese. By 1919 orientals owned nearly 16 percent of all land under irrigation in California.[10] Similar anti-Japanese legislation was passed throughout the Rocky Mountain states, and even farther east. In the wave of bad feeling that accompanied the outbreak of World War II, several additional states passed restrictions against the Japanese. These particular restrictions in all of the states have since been repealed.

Other than the early Japanese experience, and the sizable current holdings of land in Hawaii by the Japanese, there have been no periods of significant foreign investment in U.S. real estate in the twentieth century. Consequently, the early interest in statutory regulation of foreign ownership of U.S. farmland had faded away by the 1970s, and most of the states had repealed or relaxed their general restrictions.[11]

A resurgence of investment in U.S. farmland by foreign nationals during the late 1960s, which escalated throughout the 1970s, provided the stimulus for renewed restrictions against nonresident alien (NRA) ownership of farmland. Chapter 6 details these legislative restrictions.

Motives for Foreign Investment in U.S. Farmland

Timmons (1976) identifies twelve motives for foreign investment in the United States:[12]

1. Hedge against inflation
2. Safety of investment
3. Capital appreciation
4. Income flows
5. Tax advantages
6. U.S. dollar versus other currency
7. Access to resources and technology
8. Access to internal markets for products
9. Balancing investment portfolios
10. Capital and personal havens
11. Intangible benefits
12. Control factors

Motives 1, 3, 4, 5, 9, and 11 are shared with U.S. investors; motives 2, 6, 7, 8, 10, and 12 provide additional incentives for foreigners contemplating investment in U.S. real estate.

Safety of Investment

The political, economic, and defense stability of the United States is reassuring to potential investors from countries in which the safety of investment is less certain. This was aptly demonstrated by the movement of Canadian capital southward as a response to the political strife and uncertainty surrounding the proposed withdrawal of Quebec from Canada in the late 1970s.[13]

U.S. Dollar versus Other Currency

In a number of countries the prevailing currency appreciated against the U.S. dollar in the last half of the 1970s. As a result, U.S. real estate could be bought at bargain prices. Whereas prime farmland sold in the neighborhood of $2,500 to $3,000 per acre in western Europe, similar land in the United States was available for about $1,500 per acre.

Access to Resources and Technology

U.S. land may provide minerals, timber, other natural resources and accessibility to technology that are not as available in the home country of the buyer.

Access to Internal Markets

Automobiles and televisions are but two of the many products foreigners are marketing directly from production facilities situated on U.S. soil. Most foreigners who conduct farming operations in the United States also participate in the domestic market for agriculture.

Capital and Personal Havens

Certain foreign investments may represent potential avenues of escape from internal disorders or a disadvantageous investment environment in the buyer's homeland.

Control Factors

U.S. real estate may serve as a vehicle for foreigners to gain influence in relation to U.S. political or economic policy. Basically however, the behavior of the foreign investor in U.S. farmland is virtually identical to that of U.S. investors. The overwhelming majority of landowners filing under the Agricultural Foreign Investment Disclosure Act of 1978 (AFIDA) reported no intentions to change the use of the land.[14]

Many foreign owners, although absentee, retain whomever was farming the land as manager. A change of operators is reported for only about a fourth of the acreage acquired by foreigners.[15]

Proponents of Land Regulation

Given the large dollar value of foreign investment in urban real estate, one might wonder why it is that legislation is directed almost exclusively toward restricting foreign ownership of *farmland*. Farmers and farm organizations constitute the only identifiable interest groups backing such legislation.

All of the major national farmers' organizations support legislation restricting foreign ownership of U.S. farmland, although actual lobbying efforts vary widely from state to state. There is strong support at all levels for the family farm as the foundation of the highly successful U.S. agricultural system. These organizations include the National Grange, the National Farmers Union, the American Farm Bureau Federation, the National Farmers Organization, American Agri-Women, and Women Involved in Farm Economics. These groups are actively involved in lobbying efforts favoring restrictive legislation at the state level. The Ohio branches of the National Farmers Union and the American Farm Bureau, for example, supported such legislation in Ohio. In Iowa and Minnesota backing was provided by all of the major organizations, while in Louisiana the identified interest group was the Louisiana Farm Bureau. The state affiliations of the National Grange and Farmers Union and the Wisconsin Women for Agriculture supported various bills introduced into that state's legislature aimed at restricting foreign acquisition of farmland. In several states farmers, as individuals, participate in the committee hearings for such bills, regardless of their membership status in the national organizations.

The arguments invoked by these individuals and groups as justification for their stance are discussed more fully in chapter 3. Before turning attention to these arguments, the incidence and trends in domestic and foreign ownership of U.S. farmland in recent years will be examined in chapter 2.

Notes

1. Terry L. Anderson, "A Survey of Alien Land Investment in the United States, Colonial Times to Present," *Foreign Investment in U.S. Real Estate,* U.S. Department of Agriculture (hereinafter called USDA), Economics Research Service (1976), p. 11.

2. Anderson (p. 15) goes on to remark that a general naturalization policy came into existence for the colonies in 1740. There was one other way of obtaining title to lands, which was to be granted a Letter of Denization by one of the colonial governors. This practice was looked upon with disfavor by the crown as a result of the liberality of the colonial governors.

3. For further reading, consult A.M. Sakolski, *The Great American Land Bubble* (New York: Harper and Brothers, 1932) and P.W. Bidwell and J.I. Falconer, *History of Agriculture in the Northern United States 1620-1860* (New York: Peter Smith, 1941).

4. Anderson, see note , p. 12.

5. Paul W. Gates, *Landlords and Tenants on the Private Frontier* (Ithaca: Cornell University Press, 1973), pp. 7, 17, 151–2.

6. For a detailed discussion of the ebb and flow of foreign investment in the expanding American frontier, see Gilbert C. Fite, *The Farmer's Frontier 1865–1900* (Chicago: Holt, Rinehart and Winston, 1966).

7. Cleona Lewis, *America's Stake in International Investments* (Washington, D.C.: Brookings Institution, 1938), p. 81.

8. Anderson, see note 1, p. 24.

9. The several excellent accounts of land speculation in the Midwest include Paul W. Gates, *Frontier Landlords and Pioneer Tenants* (Ithaca: Cornell University Press, 1945); Leslie Hewes, *The Suitcase Farming Frontier* (Lincoln: University of Nebraska Press, 1973); Homer E. Socolofsky, *Landlord William Scully* (The Regents Press of Kansas, 1979); and Morton C. Paulson, *The Great Land Hustle* (Chicago: Henry Regnery & Co., 1972).

10. Anderson, see note 1, p. 26.

11. Fred L. Morrison and Kenneth R. Krause, *State and Federal Legal Regulation of Alien and Corporate Land Ownership and Farm Operation,* USDA, Agricultural Economic Report No. 284, pp. 14–15.

12. John Timmons, "Foreign Investment in U.S. Real Estate: An Overview," *Foreign Investment in U.S. Real Estate,* USDA, Economic Research Service (1976), pp. 5–6.

13. See also Mira Wilkens, *Foreign Enterprise in Florida* (Gainesville: University Presses of Florida, 1979), p. 32.

14. *Farmline* (June 1980), p. 6.

15. Ibid.

2

Facts and Trends in the Farmland Real Estate Market

This chapter contains numerous tables that provide overview information on two general aspects of the domestic agricultural real estate market: the structure of farmland ownership, and the nature and extent of foreign participation in it. An understanding of both aspects is a prerequisite for systematic evaluation of the economic consequences of foreign investment in U.S. farmland.

Following this overview, the structure of farmland ownership in the United States will be examined, with particular attention paid to questions such as who owns the land in the United States, how valuable the privately held land is, and what is happening to average farm size over time. In the context of this setting, that is, the preexisting structure of farmland ownership in the United States, we turn our attention to a description of foreign owners of U.S. farmland. Acreage owned, acreage bought and sold, state patterns of ownership, tenure arrangements, and country of origin are among the issues addressed. A brief overview of the findings reported by the USDA on foreign ownership of U.S. farmland within the past three years, as required under the Agricultural Foreign Investment Disclosure Act (1978), precedes the more detailed discussion.

An Overview of Foreign Investment in U.S. Farmland

As of December 31, 1982, nonresident aliens owned about 13.5 million acres of U.S. agricultural land. This represents about 0.6 percent of all land in the United States, and just above 1 percent of all privately held agricultural land.

Of the foreign-owned acreage, roughly 55 percent is in forest land, 13 percent in cropland, and 27 percent is used for pasture and other agricultural uses.

A substantial majority of the acreage is owned only in part by foreign investors; that is, the foreign interest in the land is less than 100 percent. The remaining percentage is held by U.S. entities such as corporations or partnerships.

Three-quarters of the foreign-owned acreage is owned by individuals or business entities from Canada, Netherlands Antilles, West Germany (Federal Republic of Germany), the United Kingdom, and Hong Kong.

Rhode Island is the only state with no USDA-reported, foreign-owned farmland. Elsewhere, 34 percent of the foreign holdings are in the South and 31 percent are in the West.[1]

The Structure of Farmland Ownership

The total land area of the United States is about 2.3 billion acres. The largest single owner of the land is the federal government, which owns about 34 percent (see table 2-1). That translates into roughly 762 million acres. State and local governments own an additional 6 percent of the land (136 million acres). Two percent of the land (51 million acres) is held by, or in trust for, American Indians. All figures are taken from the USDA survey of landowners in the United States (1978).[2]

The survey identified approximately 1.35 billion acres of land held by private parties (58 percent of the total). There were approximately 34 million owners: individuals, groups of individuals (such as families), and legal entities (partnerships, trusts, estates, and corporations). Table 2-2 identifies the owners of privately held land in the United States.

Two-thirds of the privately held land in the United States is owned by individuals and families, who represent by number 90 percent of all owners. Corporate owners of land tend to be few in number, but hold a much larger proportion of the private land. Family partnerships and corporations owned just under 16 percent of the land, although they comprise only about 4 percent of the owners. Altogether, individuals and families make up 94 percent of the owners, and control 82.2 percent of the land.

Most owners of private land had less than ten acres in the 1978 survey (see table 2-3). The top 0.5 percent of landowners held nearly 40 percent of

Table 2-1
Ownership of U.S. Land, 1978

	Acres (millions)	Percentage of Total Land
Federal government	762	34
State and local governments	136	6
Indian tribes and individuals	51	2
Private owners	1,350	58
Total	2,300	100

Source: USDA, Economic Research Bulletin No. 435, *Landownership in the United States, 1978*, p. 3.

Table 2–2
Owners of Privately Held U.S. Land, 1978

Type	Owners		Acres Owned	
	Thousands	Percentage	Millions	Percentage
Sole proprietorship	14,974	44.4	460.1	34.2
Family ownership	15,382	45.6	436.0	32.4
Partnership with family member(s)	1,138	3.4	143.5	10.7
Partnership with nonfamily member(s)	320	0.9	29.7	2.2
Family corporation (10 or fewer members)	220	0.6	59.2	4.3
Family corporation (10 or more members)	20	0.1	8.4	0.6
Other corporation	937	2.7	150.7	11.2
Other[a]	757	2.3	59.6	4.4
Total	33,748	100.0	1,347.2	100.0

Source: USDA, Economic Research Service Bulletin No. 435, *Landownership in the United States, 1978*, p. 14.

[a]Includes estates.

Table 2–3
Size and Distribution of U.S. Landholdings, 1978

Size (Acres)	Owners		Acres Owned	
	Thousands	Percentage	Millions	Percentage
1–9	26,485	78.5	46.2	3.4
10–49	3,300	9.8	77.7	5.8
50–69	585	1.7	33.8	2.5
70–99	820	2.4	66.9	5.0
100–139	608	1.8	69.8	5.2
140–179	568	1.7	89.7	6.7
180–259	477	1.4	102.6	7.6
260–499	522	1.5	183.4	13.6
500–999	235	0.7	160.4	11.9
1,000–1,999	88	0.3	117.1	8.6
2,000–2,999	24	0.1	57.3	4.3
3,000–4,999	17	—[a]	61.8	4.6
5,000–9,999	11	—[a]	70.5	5.2
10,000 and above	8	—[a]	210.0	15.6
Total	33,748	100.0	1,347.2	100.0

Source: USDA, Economic Research Service Bulletin No. 435, *Landownership in the United States, 1978*, p. 15.

[a]Less than 0.05 percent.

the land, while the bottom 78 percent of the owners held only 3 percent of the acreage. These owners held land in tracts of ten acres or less. The average size of a tract was about forty acres, although for those who report farming their own land the average size is about two hundred acres.

Economies of scale in production have contributed in recent decades to the well-documented increase in average farm size, decrease in numbers of farmers, and increase in farmland real estate values. Acreage expansion can be accomplished in one of two ways: purchase of additional acreage and leasing. Insofar as farmers choose to acquire additional land through purchase, farmland real estate values will climb; a result of increased demand for a static quantity. Table 2–4 chronicles the rise in farmland value since 1970, by geographic region. Predictably, the corn-belt states have experienced the largest increase in farmland values over the decade of the 1970s; roughly 335 percent. Interestingly, the western and southern states have not shown comparative rates of land-price inflation over that period, even though they experienced the highest rates of purchase by foreigners.

A comparison of the rate of increase in total net farm income from farming the land and the capital appreciation of the land itself reveals the magnitude of the farmland price inflation of the 1970s. Over the decade of the 1970s, capital gains on their land were consistently higher than farm income to operators. Everything else being equal, this trend tends to stengthen farmers' equity/debt position, which they do not realize unless their farming operations are sold. In the meantime, higher assessed values result in higher property tax assessments, which are rising faster than farm income.

Table 2–4
Per Acre Average Value of Farm Real Estate, 1970, 1975, and 1980
(1967 = 100)

Region	Mar. 1970	Mar. 1975	Feb. 1980
Northeast	135	279	472
Lake states	118	222	482
Corn belt	113	213	491
Northern plains	113	226	417
Appalachia	122	244	416
Southeast	126	257	391
Delta states	123	195	361
Southern plains	117	202	347
Mountain	125	231	388[a]
Pacific	124	180	278
Average[b]	117	213	401

Source: USDA, *Farm Real Estate Market Developments*. Economics, Statistics and Cooperative Service CD-84, August 1979, and Supplement 2, May 1980; selected pages.

[a]Excluding Nevada, New Mexico, and Utah, because of lack of data.

[b]Excluding Alaska and Hawaii.

The steady increase in average farm size and the decrease in numbers of farms over the past four decades is documented in table 2–5. From 1940 to 1974, the total number of farms fell by more than 62 percent, from 6,102 units to 2,314. The number of acres of farmland in production fell less dramatically over that same period, from 1,065 million acres to 1,017 million acres; a decline of 4.5 percent. One would thus expect average farm size to have increased over the 1940–1974 period, and it has. Per-farm acreage has more than doubled since 1940, from an average of 216 acres to 440 acres.

Most of the landowners in the United States live in the states where their holdings are located (see table 2–6). Over 90 percent of the owners live in the same state, and 92 percent of these owners reside in the same county in which their land is located. Farmers may, of course, own a single tract of land that falls into two (or more) counties. On the other hand, as mentioned briefly earlier, farmers who desire to expand the quantity of acreage they farm in order to fully realize all scale economies may rent additional acreage, which may or may not adjoin their own tracts. Thus, statistics on average farm size may understate the average acreage farmed by an operator, if

Table 2–5
Number of Farms, Land in Farms, and Size of Farm, by Tenure of Operator

	Year								
	1920	*1930*	*1940*	*1950*	*1954*	*1959*	*1964*	*1969*	*1974*
Number of farms *(thousands)*									
Full owners[a]	3,437	2,969	3,122	3,115	2,758	2,139	1,836	1,706	1,424
Part owners	559	657	616	826	857	811	782	672	628
Tenants	2,459	2,669	2,365	1,447	1,168	760	540	353	262
Total	6,454	6,295	6,102	5,388	4,783	3,708	3,158	2,730	2,314
Land in farms *(millions of acres)*									
Full owners[a]	N.A.[b]	436	451	526	495	458	432	375	359
Part owners	N.A.	247	301	423	470	498	533	551	535
Tenants	N.A.	307	313	212	193	167	145	138	122
Total	959	990	1,065	1,161	1,158	1,123	1,110	1,063	1,017
Size of farm *(acres)*									
Full owners[a]	N.A.	128	124	136	145	165	175	220	252
Part owners	N.A.	375	489	512	549	614	682	819	852
Tenants	N.A.	115	132	147	165	220	268	390	467
Total	149	157	175	216	242	303	352	389	440

Source: USDA Handbook No. 551, *1978 Handbook of Agricultural Charts* (Washington, D.C.: U.S. Government Printing Office, 1979), p. 26.
[a]Includes managers.
[b]N.A. = not available.

Table 2–6
Residence of U.S. Landowners in Relation to Landholding

Residence	Owners[a]		Acres Owned	
	Thousands	Percentage	Millions	Percentage
In same country as land	27,687.8	86.7	845.6	76.6
In same state, different country from land	2,334.8	7.4	159.6	14.5
In another state from land	924.9	2.8	64.9	5.8
In another country from land	25.7	0.1	0.4	0.0
No response	944.8	3.0	34.2	3.1
Total	31,918.0	100.0	1,104.7	100.0

Source: USDA, Economic Research Service Bulletin No. 435, *Landownership in the United States, 1978*, p. 17.

[a]Excludes corporations and other business entities.

owner-operators also maintain lease arrangements to any considerable extent. Note that only 0.1 percent of the owners live in another country, representing a negligible fraction of the acreage. Of the one-half of one percent of the private land owned by foreigners in the United States, apparently most of that land is owned by resident (as opposed to nonresident) aliens.

Over three-fourths of the landowners in the 1978 USDA survey had no direct connection with agricultural activities (see table 2–7). Twenty-five

Table 2–7
Tenure of U.S. Landdowners, 1978

Tenure	Owners		Acres Owned	
	Thousands	Percentage	Millions	Percentage
Full-owner operator	2,451.2	7.3	336.7	25.0
Full-owner operator landlord	313.5	1.0	70.5	5.2
Part-owner operator	870.5	2.6	252.2	18.7
Part-owner operator landlord	51.2	0.2	30.0	2.2
Tenant-owner operator	823.7	2.4	9.0	0.9
Nonoperator	26,702.9	79.0	344.6	25.5
Nonoperator landlord	2,535.0	7.5	304.2	22.7
Total	33,748.0	100.0	1,347.2	100.0

Source: USDA, Economic Research Service Bulletin No. 435, *Landownership in the United States, 1978*, p. 16.

percent of the land was owned by full-owner operators, who comprised just over 7 percent of the owners. Slightly more than 2.5 million owners were nonfarm operators who rented out about three-fourths of their total acreage. Although they operate none of their own acreage, tenant farmers owned about 9 million acres, and rented just over a third of that to others. Just over one-half of all acreage owned is held by nonoperators, who would rent the land out.

U.S. citizens make up well over 90 percent of the landowners in the United States (see table 2–8), and own 95 percent of the privately held land. The single largest group of foreigners owning land in the United States is Canadian; no other single country owns enough land to appear as a measurable percent. Foreigners are shown as owning only 0.2 percent of the privately held land, considerably less than the 0.5 percent that is the currently established figure. No doubt, the figures listed are somewhat misleading, in that the figures for U.S. citizens probably include U.S. corporations that are partially owned by foreigners. In addition, the nonresponse category probably includes a high percentage of foreigners, who desire anonymity in their purchase behavior.

**The Nature and Extent of Foreign Ownership
of U.S. Farmland**

Table 2–9 lists agricultural landholdings of foreign owners, by state, as of December 1982. Foreigners own no acreage in Rhode Island, and less than one thousand acres in Alaska, Connecticut, and Massachusetts. The largest number of acres owned by foreign persons was reported in Maine. Fourteen percent of the privately held land in Maine is owned by foreigners, with some 96 percent of the foreign-owned acreage in the possession of three large timber companies. After Maine, the next three largest states in terms of the proportion of private land owned by foreigners are South Carolina,

**Table 2–8
Citizenship of U.S. Landowners, 1978**

Citizenship	Owners		Acres Owned	
	Thousands	*Percentage*	*Millions*	*Percentage*
U.S. citizen	29,793.6	93.2	1,049.6	95.0
Canadian	52.7	0.2	0.4	0.1
Other	88.9	0.3	0.8	0.1
No response	1,982.8	6.3	53.9	4.8
Total	31,918.0	100.0	1,104.7	100.0

Source: USDA, Economic Research Service Bulletin No. 435, *Landownership in the United States, 1978*, p. 18.

Table 2–9
Agricultural Landholdings of Foreign Owners, by State (December 1982)

State	Total Land Area of State (thousands of acres)	Privately Owned Agricultural Land (thousands of acres)	Foreign-Owned Agricultural Land (acres)	Percentage
Alabama	32,491	29,467	590,145	2.0
Alaska	365,333	400	753	0.2
Arizona	72,645	10,983	225,755	2.1
Arkansas	33,330	28,834	116,401	0.4
California	100,031	47,353	898,711	1.9
Colorado	66,301	37,527	461,796	1.2
Connecticut	3,118	2,267	801	neg.
Delaware	1,236	1,064	8,051	0.8
Florida	34,658	26,529	491,723	1.9
Georgia	37,156	33,253	944,154	2.8
Hawaii	4,112	1,992	56,374	2.8
Idaho	52,744	15,166	165,594	1.1
Illinois	35,613	32,326	148,774	0.5
Indiana	22,996	20,909	95,581	0.5
Iowa	35,818	33,912	35,529	0.1
Kansas	52,338	49,911	68,003	0.1
Kentucky	25,388	22,915	40,403	0.2
Louisiana	28,494	26,463	147,807	0.6
Maine	19,837	18,829	2,658,669	14.1
Maryland	6,295	5,146	44,492	0.9
Massachusetts	5,007	3,322	442	neg.
Michigan	36,450	26,117	192,012	0.7
Minnesota	50,911	36,204	103,218	0.3
Mississippi	30,229	26,629	336,661	1.3
Missouri	44,125	40,025	61,721	0.2
Montana	93,048	54,189	347,810	0.6
Nebraska	49,052	45,397	85,348	0.2
Nevada	70,332	7,586	70,147	0.9
New Hampshire	5,756	4,682	103,166	2.2
New Jersey	4,780	2,894	23,988	0.8
New Mexico	77,654	34,451	661,744	1.9
New York	30,321	24,257	358,384	1.5
North Carolina	31,259	27,321	268,728	1.0
North Dakota	44,351	39,617	19,205	neg.
Ohio	26,243	22,979	43,902	0.2
Oklahoma	43,939	38,875	28,435	0.1
Oregon	61,558	25,685	527,400	2.1
Pennsylvania	28,728	22,380	158,785	0.7
Rhode Island	675	439	0	neg.
South Carolina	19,330	15,932	507,140	3.2
South Dakota	48,609	38,241	41,379	0.1
Tennessee	26,339	22,901	347,395	1.5
Texas	167,691	156,768	912,784	0.6
Utah	52,527	10,779	239,445	2.2
Vermont	5,935	5,251	94,318	1.8
Virginia	25,411	21,499	127,353	0.6
Washington	42,567	23,028	398,411	1.7
West Virginia	15,436	13,744	58,240	0.4
Wisconsin	34,833	27,637	18,664	neg.
Wyoming	62,073	26,142	123,563	0.5

Source: USDA, *Foreign Ownership of U.S. Agricultural Land: through December 31, 1982*, Economi Research Service (1983), p. 8.

Table 2–10
Foreign Owners of U.S. Agricultural Landholdings, by State (December 1982)

State	Individual		Corporation	
	Parcels	Acres	Parcels	Acres
Alabama	13	798	376	589,347
Alaska	0	0	3	753
Arizona	40	9,925	220	215,830
Arkansas	52	23,513	87	92,888
California	272	69,234	872	829,477
Colorado	123	117,469	200	344,327
Connecticut	4	105	10	696
Delaware	6	1,612	8	6,439
Florida	526	27,038	753	464,685
Georgia	128	44,994	656	899,160
Hawaii	23	7,301	28	49,073
Idaho	23	6,523	37	159,071
Illinois	46	10,734	302	138,040
Indiana	28	4,808	239	90,773
Iowa	70	16,898	57	18,631
Kansas	23	4,979	64	63,024
Kentucky	30	5,398	70	35,005
Louisiana	10	7,749	92	140,058
Maine	25	15,126	68	2,643,543
Maryland	44	7,520	116	36,972
Massachusetts	3	12	4	430
Michigan	64	5,280	52	186,732
Minnesota	35	16,146	53	87,072
Mississippi	8	937	162	335,724
Missouri	28	9,740	86	51,981
Montana	88	31,287	84	316,523
Nebraska	9	2,885	34	82,463
Nevada	11	115	16	70,032
New Hampshire	8	1,415	19	101,751
New Jersey	10	481	74	23,507
New Mexico	37	584	31	661,160
New York	502	31,861	145	326,523
North Carolina	48	9,126	339	259,602
North Dakota	45	13,302	14	5,903
Ohio	36	6,581	290	37,321
Oklahoma	9	1,040	60	27,395
Oregon	41	7,839	65	519,561
Pennsylvania	24	2,098	68	156,687
South Carolina	17	4,429	884	502,711
South Dakota	36	11,072	28	30,307
Tennessee	66	15,847	208	331,548
Texas	530	167,351	874	745,433
Utah	515	21,469	36	217,976
Vermont	693	32,000	222	62,318
Virginia	95	22,543	222	104,810
Washington	527	48,425	426	349,986
West Virginia	19	3,140	25	55,100
Wisconsin	55	10,229	26	8,435
Wyoming	2	500	25	123,063

Source: USDA, *Foreign Ownership of U.S. Agricultural Land: through December 31, 1982*, Economic Research Service (1983), p. 11.

Georgia, and Hawaii. In a total of nine states, including the ones listed here, more than 2 percent of their private land is owned by foreigners.

The distribution of landownership between individuals and corporations, in terms of number of parcels and acreage owned by foreigners, is presented in table 2-10. Corporations own the bulk of the acreage in virtually every state, and corporate ownership is more common than ownership by individuals.

In some respects, measurement of foreign ownership of U.S. agricultural land is a chicken-and-egg problem. None of the midwestern farming states have a significant portion of their land under foreign ownership. Is this because regulations have proven so effective, or have regulations been enacted in spite of the small incidence of foreign ownership of farmland in those states? We shall return to answer this question, at least partially.

Landholdings by foreigners tend to be concentrated in the hands of a few owners (see table 2-11). Individuals tend to own smaller parcels, by a factor of nearly one hundred, than parcels owned by corporations. Seventy percent of the foreign owners have tracts of three hundred acres or less, an amount that totals less than 3 percent of the foreign-owned land. The 30 percent of the owners holding three hundred or more acres own 97 percent of the foreign-owned acreage.

The public concern over foreign investment in U.S. farmland during the latter 1970s coincided with the upsurge of foreign purchases of U.S. farmland during that time period (see table 2-12). The pre-1975 period is characterized by relatively modest buying by foreigners during the 1960s, accompanied by a slight upswing during the first half of the 1970s. In terms of numbers of parcels bought and numbers of acres purchased, foreign participation in the U.S. farmland market mushroomed during the last half of the 1970s and into the first years of the 1980s. Between 1975 and 1981, for

Table 2-11
Foreign-Owned U.S. Agricultural Landholdings, by Size of Holding (December 1982)

Size (acres)	Owners (number)	Parcels (number)	Acres (number)
Less than 20	2,152	2,262	15,726
20–59	1,336	1,538	47,120
60–99	670	890	52,253
100–299	1,476	1,952	258,965
300–999	1,393	2,083	779,040
1,000 or more	1,008	5,164	12,307,924
Total	8,035	13,889	13,461,028

Source: USDA, Economic Research Service (1983), *Foreign Ownership of U.S. Agricultural Land: through December 31, 1982*, p. 12.

Table 2–12

Foreign-Owned U.S. Agricultural Landholdings, by Date of Acquisition

Date Acquired	Parcels (number)	Acres (number)	Average Acreage
1982[a]	957	576,190	602.1
1981	1,846	3,132,464	1,696.9
1980	1,769	1,424,503	805.3
1979	2,176	2,408,960	1,107.1
1978	1,603	692,414	431.9
1977	1,134	753,202	664.2
1976	767	533,449	695.5
1975	493	274,743	557.3
1970–1974	1,437	882,781	614.3
1960–1969	1,122	1,301,629	1,160.1
Before 1960	579	1,461,979	2,525.0

Source: USDA, Economic Research Service (1983), *Foreign Ownership of U.S. Agricultural Land: through December 31, 1982*, p. 13.

[a]Data on 1982 filings under the Agricultural Foreign Investment Disclosure Act are incomplete. There is an approximate six-month time lag on filings with the USDA. Thus, the figures listed understate true acquisitions by foreigners in 1982.

example, the number of parcels bought by foreigners increased almost fourfold, and acreage purchased jumped more than tenfold. In terms of adjusted current value of holdings, foreigners bought more than fifteen times as much land in 1981 than they did in 1975.[3]

Nearly 13.5 million acres of land were reportedly held by foreigners in 1982. Of that total, roughly 63 percent was held by U.S. corporations with some foreign interest. Foreign persons not connected in any way with a U.S. corporation held the other 37 percent. Table 2–13 lists the ten largest foreign countries, in terms of number of acres owned of U.S. agricultural land, as well as the ten largest countries in which joint U.S.-foreign corporations have purchased U.S. farmland. U.S. corporations with Canadian interests own about 20 percent of the total foreign-owned acreage. When the acreage owned by Canadians who are unconnected in any manner with U.S. corporations is included, the percentage of U.S. farmland owned by Canadians rises to thirty. Seventy-five percent of the foreign-owned acreage is owned by five countries: Canada, the United Kingdom, Hong Kong, West Germany, and the Netherlands Antilles. This immediately sets one myth at rest—Arab sheiks are not major landowners in the United States.

Table 2–14 details the method of payment utilized by foreign purchasers of U.S. farmland. Nearly half of all purchases are by cash only, a much higher percentage than among domestic buyers. Nearly one-third of the purchases are by credit only, although the sources of credit are not specified. Foreign buyers undoubtedly patronize foreign sources of credit, as well as U.S. sources.

Table 2–13

U.S. Agricultural Landholdings, by Country of Foreign Owner: Ten Largest Individual and Joint Owners (December 1982)

Country	Owners (number)	Parcels (number)	Acres (number)
Individual Owners			
Canada	2,688	3,104	1,445,109
W. Germany	1,015	1,471	675,151
Netherlands Antilles	397	511	531,966
United Kingdom	191	256	380,783
Switzerland	256	347	236,703
Mexico	224	301	211,106
Hong Kong	35	60	175,776
Panama	134	185	148,732
Netherlands	442	687	136,207
Japan	28	32	112,056
Joint Owners			
U.S./Canada	272	933	2,655,659
U.S./Hong Kong	8	70	1,691,629
U.S./U.K.	118	1,686	1,504,636
U.S./Neth. Antilles	114	192	507,643
U.S./W. Germany	189	366	480,480
U.S./France	52	209	304,436
U.S./Luxembourg	23	31	236,079
U.S./Netherlands	85	575	227,555
U.S./Switzerland	130	249	185,189
U.S./Italy	13	15	76,753

Source: USDA, Economic Research Service (1983), *Foreign Ownership of U.S. Agricultural Land: through December 31, 1982*, pp. 16–18.

Table 2–14

Foreign-Owned U.S. Agricultural Landholdings, by Method of Acquisition (December 1982)

Method	Parcels (number)	Acres (number)
Cash only	6,529	4,592,105
Credit only	4,834	2,787,498
Trade only	283	217,220
Gift inheritance only	371	227,385
Foreclosure only	23	8,965
Other method only	345	2,235,537
Cash and credit only	1,179	986,042
Cash and trade only	135	2,158,097
Cash and any other combination	45	11,393
No report	60	38,010
Noncash combinations	85	198,776
Total	13,889	13,461,028

Source: USDA, *Foreign Ownership of U.S. Agricultural Land: through December 31, 1982*, Economic Research Service (1983), p. 43.

There does not appear to be a tendency for foreign owners to remove agricultural land from production or to significantly alter the pre-existing crop patterns. No change in tenure was reported for 42 percent of the total foreign-owned acreage; 29 percent reported some change of tenure arrangements. Foreign owners generally tend to either run the farm operation themselves or to lease the land under a crop or cash lease (see table 2-15). Of the acreage for which reports were received, well over 90 percent fell into one of these two categories. Note that over 50 percent of the foreign-owned agricultural land apparently is farmed by resident aliens, with the remainder leased out.

A glance at data on acquisitions and dispositions of U.S. agricultural land by foreigners over the 1979–1982 period provides some indication of the trend of foreign participation in the domestic farmland market. With respect to the number of parcels acquired over this time period, the pace of foreign investment has remained relatively constant, although the distribution of such investment among the states varied somewhat (see table 2-16). The sharp drop in number of parcels reported as purchased in 1982 as com-

Table 2-15
Tenure of Foreign-Owned U.S. Agricultural Landholdings
(December 1982)

Tenure	Parcels	Acreage
Current		
Foreign owner	4,728	6,810,962
Manager	1,103	716,928
Tenant	4,724	3,187,573
No report	3,326	2,736,233
Total	13,889	13,461,028
Rental		
Crop	1,727	684,005
Cash	3,273	2,646,520
Both	94	98,056
No report	4,067	3,221,485
Not applicable	4,728	6,810,962
Total	13,889	13,461,028
Intended change		
None	5,332	5,666,209
New	4,896	3,805,806
Both	40	32,794
No report	3,621	3,956,219
Total	13,889	13,461,028

Source: USDA, *Foreign Ownership of U.S. Agricultural Land: through December 31, 1982*, Economic Research Service (1983), p. 32.

Table 2–16

Acquisitions of U.S. Agricultural Land by Foreigners, by State

State	Feb. 2, 1979–Dec. 31, 1980		Jan. 1, 1981–Dec. 31, 1981		Jan. 1, 1982 Dec. 31, 1982	
	Parcels	Acreage	Parcels	Acreage	Parcels	Acreag
Alabama	111	64,631	61	322,421	28	13,08
Alaska	1	96	0	0	0	
Arizona	111	72,461	29	4,943	11	3,70
Arkansas	50	41,861	21	14,486	13	8,52
California	353	267,017	102	66,042	65	22,21
Colorado	91	120,547	52	100,261	37	83,67
Connecticut	3	301	2	50	0	
Delaware	5	940	2	356	0	
Florida	294	102,857	113	69 777	67	13,89
Georgia	208	103,114	143	447,516	126	47,05
Hawaii	10	7,806	2	39	2	30
Idaho	8	7,095	3	811	2	46
Illinois	78	22,398	60	12,830	20	3,18
Indiana	85	10,547	26	11,065	26	45
Iowa	44	9,466	1	30	0	
Kansas	27	21,422	3	1,825	2	93
Kentucky	17	7,657	9	2,864	5	2,60
Louisiana	47	59,028	4	1,925	6	4,15
Maine	4	4,891	22	888,118	5	16,99
Maryland	46	12,937	12	1,919	18	3,71
Massachusetts	1	15,000	0	0	1	
Michigan	22	3,092	5	552	8	142,07
Minnesota	9	480	8	1,305	2	4
Mississippi	58	47,818	16	201,887	6	3,48
Missouri	17	5,890	4	1,115	1	53
Montana	14	97,524	14	16,389	6	21,38
Nebraska	7	1,252	1	160	1	6,96
Nevada	6	47,469	3	1,380	0	
New Hampshire	3	1,201	0	0	1	10
New Jersey	21	3,408	6	70	7	63
New Mexico	6	8,968	5	107,525	3	80
New York	87	21,346	55	10,044	43	25,57
North Carolina	65	44,840	45	15,122	55	20,26
North Dakota	2	1,016	0	0	0	
Ohio	30	10,274	15	4,977	13	2,68
Oklahoma	8	1,811	2	3,348	1	2,14
Oregon	19	3,215	16	113,680	6	41
Pennsylvania	12	1,766	6	1,125	3	11
South Carolina	194	64,017	210	114,289	157	38,68
South Dakota	17	21,238	7	1,740	2	16
Tennessee	43	30,439	36	18,388	26	7,17
Texas	407	277,016	185	52,942	107	58,88
Utah	237	10,344	10	6,104	4	24
Vermont	148	14,919	49	3,943	23	2,52
Virginia	122	47,457	43	10,512	31	8,15
Washington	174	9,140	45	250,883	9	68
West Virginia	12	2,393	1	105	4	6,65
Wisconsin	19	4,868	8	868	4	73
Wyoming	3	5,668	3	2,606	0	
Total	3,358	1,740,544	1,455	2,888,237	752	504,27

Source: USDA, *Foreign Ownership of U.S. Agricultural Land* (February 2, 1979–December 31, 198 through December 31, 1981; and through December 31, 1982). Economic Research Service; selected page

pared with the previous three years is due to an extended time lag in filing under the AFIDA requirements by foreign investors. In terms of the number of acres purchased, however, foreign investment increased substantially in 1981 over 1979 and 1980, before falling off again in 1982. Foreigners bought no land in Rhode Island, and negligible quantities of acreage in Iowa, North Dakota, and most of the New England states. The well-documented pattern of foreign investment in the South and West is evident, both in terms of numbers of buyers and acreage purchased.

Over this four-year period, sales of U.S. farmland by foreign owners also remained relatively constant (see table 2-17). Roughly 325 parcels have been sold per year by foreign owners since 1979, about one quarter as many parcels as were purchased by foreigners. Parcels sold averaged 737 acres, while tracts bought averaged 922 acres. This latter figure is slightly misleading, however, because it is raised considerably by several very large purchases of forest land in Maine by foreign companies in 1981. Corporations from Canada and West Germany were the most active sellers.

Table 2-18 identifies purchasers of foreign-owned U.S. land. Nearly 50 percent of the parcels, and well over 50 percent of the acreage sold during the 1979-1982 period were purchased by U.S. citizens.

Concluding Comments

Calculations of *net* acquisitions of U.S. agricultural land by foreigners must, of course, take into account the quantity of land disposed by foreigners each year to U.S. buyers. At present rates of net investment, it would take foreigners over twenty years to acquire an additional 1 percent of U.S. farmland. Foreign participation in the U.S. farmland market is insufficient, by itself, to account for any significant proportion of the farmland price inflation of the 1970s. Half of the foreign owners are resident operators; the rest lease out their land or hire managers to conduct the farming operation, under arrangements that differ little from those prevailing in the U.S. agricultural community. In short, there is no specific reason to believe that foreign investment constitutes a significant fraction of total investment in U.S. farmland each year, in terms of numbers of buyers, quantities of acreage bought, or in behavior of purchasers.

Table 2-17

Dispositions of U.S. Agricultural Land by Foreigners, by State

State	Feb. 2, 1979–Dec. 31, 1980		Jan. 1, 1981–Dec. 31, 1981		Jan. 1, 1982–Dec. 31, 1982	
	Parcels	Acres	Parcels	Acres	Parcels	Acres
Alabama	13	20,230	8	6,841	17	1,58
Arizona	25	5,082	20	1,257	22	5,89
Arkansas	11	13,909	7	3,948	0	
California	77	113,202	24	50,404	11	5,09
Colorado	28	33,430	21	109,733	10	30,62
Florida	77	33,951	33	4,373	21	1,68
Georgia	47	6,478	28	11,359	42	14,39
Hawaii	0	0	1	35	0	
Idaho	7	5,979	0	0	2	30
Illinois	27	4,727	3	323	6	59
Indiana	29	4,927	11	10,092	2	1,03
Iowa	2	685	5	517	0	
Kentucky	3	149	0	0	1	33
Louisiana	16	25,281	10	3,733	2	8,26
Maine	0	0	2	15,569	1	11,05
Maryland	3	1,159	0	0	3	30
Michigan	3	297	0	0	0	
Minnesota	2	721	0	0	6	57
Mississippi	9	5,322	3	777	0	
Missouri	7	4,665	2	1,421	2	3,93
Montana	6	56,068	1	237	1	
Nebraska	2	647	2	320	0	
Nevada	2	153,312	8	666	0	
New Hampshire	1	128	0	0	0	
New Jersey	8	382	8	666	0	
New Mexico	0	0	0	0	1	3,60
New York	13	1,531	4	83	6	64
North Carolina	20	6,402	1	1,543	16	11,83
Ohio	8	3,003	0	0	0	
Oklahoma	2	575	8	3,032	4	38
Oregon	8	1,668	2	13,446	2	25
Pennsylvania	2	216	1	32	0	
South Carolina	29	7,213	12	1,192	7	38
South Dakota	0	0	4	554	0	
Tennessee	9	4,337	5	4,605	11	1,83
Texas	72	31,654	47	22,485	54	19,42
Utah	9	86	8	234	9	42
Vermont	46	2,112	21	1,282	10	38
Virginia	10	1,663	8	667	15	3,51
Washington	40	1,611	11	337	3	2
West Virginia	0	0	0	0	1	6
Wisconsin	12	1,898	3	213	0	
Wyoming	2	2,351	1	1,600	0	
Total	687	557,053	325	272,910	288	128,45

Source: USDA, *Foreign Ownership of U.S. Agricultural Land* (February 1, 1979–December 31, 198 through December 31, 1981; and through December 31, 1982). Economic Research Service; select pages.

Table 2-18

Citizenship of Buyers of Foreign-Owned U.S. Agricultural Land

Purchaser	Feb. 2, 1979–Dec. 31, 1980		Jan. 2, 1981–Dec. 31, 1981		Jan. 1, 1982—Dec. 31, 1982	
	Parcels	Acres	Parcels	Acres	Parcels	Acres
U.S.	337	336,213	191	193,537	129	63,241
Foreign	215	159,177	76	50,618	97	45,702
Unknown	125	51,957	50	24,979	54	16,363
No report	9	9,696	7	3,741	7	3,115
Combination	1	10	1	35	1	30
Total	687	557,053	325	272,910	288	128,451

Source: USDA, *Foreign Ownership of U.S. Agricultural Land* (February 2, 1979–December 31, 1980; through December 31, 1981; and through December 31, 1982). Economic Research Service; selected pages.

Notes

1. USDA, *Foreign Ownership of U.S. Agricultural Land: through December 31, 1982* (Washington, D.C.: U.S. Govt. Printing Office, 1983), p. vii.

2. USDA, Bulletin No. 435, *Landownership in the United States, 1978* (Washington, D.C.: U.S. Govt. Printing Office, 1979).

3. USDA, (see note 1), p. 13.

3 Economic Impacts of Foreign Investment in U.S. Farmland

Widespread state limitations on foreign participation in the U.S. farm real estate market seem to imply that U.S. farmers suffer adverse consequences as a result of the foreign presence in the domestic farmland market. Such an adverse impact, assuming it exists, could not result from large-scale ownership of U.S. farmland by nonresident aliens—recall the documentation in chapter 2 to the effect that foreigners owned less than one-half of one percent of all privately owned U.S. farmland. Is it the case then, that despite the relatively minute incidence of land ownership, foreigners impose significant, negative externalities on domestic farmers or other identifiable interest groups?

A number of researchers have directed their attention to this question in the late 1970s and early 1980s. Across a broad spectrum of suspected impacts of foreign ownership of U.S. farmland, findings of these researchers support one conclusion unanimously: foreign ownership per se, of U.S. agricultural land, has a negligible impact on U.S. farmers.

In this chapter I address the topic of the economic impact of foreign investment in U.S. farmland.[1] As suggested by Jansma, et al. (1981), such impacts may occur at the microeconomic and/or macroeconomic level.[2] In this chapter reasons for evaluating the impact of foreign investment in U.S. farmland separately from other types of foreign investment are discussed, and sources of information about foreign investment are detailed. Then I will explore the proposed and empirically evident microeconomic impacts of foreign investment, and conclude the chapter with the macroeconomic consequences of such investment.

Unique Aspects of Farmland

Foreign investment in U.S. agricultural land represents a small fraction of total foreign investment in the United States. In terms of dollar value of assets, investment by foreigners in urban real estate is many times greater than in agricultural land. Yet investigators normally treat agricultural real estate separately from other types of real estate for purposes of analysis. The justification for this methodology, as presented by Jansma, et al. (1981) takes one of three forms: the *infinite-life* argument, the total-supply-of-land-is-fixed argument, and the immobility-of-land argument.

The infinite-life argument is that land is eternal (since it does not depreciate), hence profits from working the land can be siphoned off to a foreign country forever. Yet other nonfarmland assets may also have an infinite life, or its near equivalent, so it is unclear that foreigners would favor U.S. farmland over other types of portfolio investment for this reason. Moreover, the historical record clearly demonstrates that foreigners frequently enter the domestic real estate market as sellers as well as buyers, and also seek to obtain U.S. citizenship.[3] The infinite-life argument is therefore untenable as a criterion for treating U.S. farmland in a fashion that differs from other types of foreign investment.

The argument that the supply of land is fixed also is inadequate to justify separate treatment of agricultural land. Certain investments in land (such as irrigation and draining) can marginally increase the supply of what Jansma and colleagues (1981) term "effective" farmland. The argument that sales to foreigners of U.S. land necessarily decrease sales to U.S. citizens by an equal amount is thus tenuous at best, resting on a restrictive definition of farmland as constituting the natural, untampered-with attributes of the land.

Immobility is the truly unique characteristic of land. Most factors of production can be moved to take advantage of locational quasi rents; land cannot. Thus, productivity is dependent on soil, weather, and other natural conditions specific to the location of the tract. Moreover, there are interdependencies between a given tract of farmland and its "economic neighbors."[4] An analysis of the impact of foreign investment must therefore be more comprehensive in the agricultural sector than elsewhere.

Sources of Information about Foreign
Ownership of U.S. Real Estate

Before one can begin to quantify the economic impact of foreign investment in U.S. farmland, one has to have access to reliable sources of information regarding not only the behavior of foreigners, but also the behavior of U.S. farmers and trends in the farmland real estate market as a whole, general movements in agricultural prices, and more.

Detailed information on agricultural prices (crops, debt, farmland, and so on) is available on a continuously updated basis through the U.S. Department of Agriculture. More general information on inflation rates, unemployment rates, age, income, and other pertinent variables can be gleaned from sources such as *Statistical Abstract, Historical Statistics of the United States,* and the Bureau of Labor Statistics. Friedman (1979) suggests seven potential sources of information about foreign investors: (1) real estate brokers, (2) real estate appraisers, (3) counselors, (4) lending institutions, (5) property managers, (6) tax assessors and collectors, and (7) records of ownership.[5]

Real Estate Brokers

It is unlikely that real estate brokers would voluntarily supply detailed information about foreign investors or the properties owned by foreign investors. Leaks of such information can hurt their business in two ways. First, anonymity is sometimes valuable to the foreign investor, who would patronize brokerage firms with established records of refusing to impart information about clients. Second, disclosure of such information might increase the likelihood that a competing broker would approach the prospective buyer or seller with an alternative deal. Moreover, if real estate brokers were willing to disclose information, the accuracy of their data would be open to question, since the agents themselves are often unaware of the true identities of purchasers.

Real Estate Appraisers

Appraisals are nearly always required by third-party lenders before they agree to commit funds secured by real estate. Purchasers (foreign or domestic) may also contract for sale of property contingent on appraised market value equaling or exceeding the contractual sales price. Although real estate appraisers are cooperative about sharing information with one another, the accuracy of their data with respect to total foreign investment is less than ideal. Not only are appraisals not involved in every real estate transaction, appraisers also may not necessarily know the true identity or nationality of the purchasers.

Counselors

Counselors are essentially real estate consultants, whose knowledge about foreign investments could be quite great. However, the quality of their information is suspect for the same reasons applied to appraisers.

Lending Institutions

Lending institutions are also an inadequate source of information regarding the extent of foreign ownership of U.S. real estate. They have no information on those foreigners who either pay in cash or obtain financing from outside the United States. They have limited information on foreign investors who assume existing mortgages without revealing their nationality and on foreigners who arrange financing while concealing their country of origin and identity.

Property Managers

Managers of properties owned by foreign aliens are a potential source of information about their employers, local rental rates, land tenure effects, conservation efforts, size of holdings, and other pertinent questions. The manager and/or the absentee owner would, of course, be concerned about the disclosure of such information, for a variety of reasons (such as higher tax assessments or problems for owners with their own governments). If the foreign-owned property is held by a U.S. trustee who is ignorant of the owner's identity, some information could be obtained, although it would likely be incomplete.

Tax Assessors and Collectors

Tax assessors in each county of the United States are notified by the deed recorders of every recorded ownership change. Since foreign investors often have U.S. intermediaries (trustees, banks, attorneys) to pay property tax bills and purchase properties, tax assessors and collectors may not know the identities of the owners. In addition, recorded documents do not indicate actual purchase price in most states, and assessed values do not reflect fair market value of the property for time lag reasons (among others).[6] Thus, tax assessors and collectors would probably be poor sources of information on the extent of foreign ownership of farmland in the United States.

Ownership Records

Real estate ownership records are filed in each county. However, the identity of foreign owners of U.S. farmland may be obscured through interposing trustees, wholly or partially owned subsidiaries, or other agents between themselves and the name on the deed.[7] As a monitoring device, ownership records cannot define accurately the scope of foreign investment in U.S. agricultural land.

In terms of more general studies of foreign ownership, six efforts have appeared since 1975; four seek to determine the extent of foreign investment in U.S. farmland, and the fifth and sixth attempt to shed empirical light on the impact of foreign ownership.

The ongoing monitoring of foreign investment in U.S. farmland required under the AFIDA (1978) provides the best source of continuing information about the extent of foreign ownership of agricultural lands. The act requires the Secretary of Agriculture to monitor (identify) nonresident foreign owners of agricultural land (including forest and timber lands) in the United States. Individuals and corporations (and other legal interests) maintaining at least a 5-percent interest in the entity holding title to the land are required to report under the act. The Secretary of Agriculture is further required to analyze and report the impact of foreign ownership on family farms and rural communities. The report for the year ending December 31, 1982 indicates that foreign individuals and entities held 13.5 million acres of U.S. agricultural land.[8]

The first serious empirical examination into the extent of foreign ownership came in 1975. The Department of Commerce surveyed six thousand foreign owners of real estate (some of which was not farmland). Based on this survey, the Commerce Department estimated that foreign-held U.S. land amounted to roughly 4.9 million acres. The estimate is likely to understate the true incidence however, since inclusion in the survey sample was predicted upon ownership of at least two hundred acres.

In 1978, the General Accounting Office published the results of a study conducted through that office entitled *Foreign Ownership of U.S. Farmland: Much Concern, Little Data* (see note 7). Although their data are based on confirmed cases of foreign ownership in twenty-five counties covering parts of five states, their study suffers from the same (under)reporting problems as the Commerce Department study, and estimated incidence of foreign ownership is probably biased downward.

Aside from the USDA reports, the most recent investigation of the incidence of foreign ownership of U.S. farmland is the study requested by the Senate Agriculture Committee. Published in January 1979, this report surveyed members of the Cooperative Extension Service and USDA's Agricultural Stabilization and Cooperation Service for each of the fifty states.

A follow-up to this so-called Talmadge Report was conducted by Jansma, et al. (1981) for their widely cited report on the impact of foreign investment in U.S. farmland. They surveyed Extension agents in thirty-one counties in eighteen states—counties in which a "higher-than-average" level of foreign investment activity was reported. Sample responses received from twenty-four counties in fourteen states shed some light on the implications of foreign ownership for land-use intensity, prices paid for farmland, and numerous related issues.

Researchers at Iowa State University, under contract from the USDA, conducted a survey of operators of foreign-owned farmland tracts in twenty-one counties in Iowa, California, and Mississippi for the 1979 crop year. They compared operators on foreign-owned farms with operators of locally owned and non-locally owned farms, and with owner-operators, in an effort to determine any differences in farm use among classes of operators.

Microeconomic Consequences of
Foreign Ownership

Jansma, et al. (1981) recognize four specific areas in which farmers may suffer adverse consequences from foreign participation in the agricultural community: (1) price, size, and availability of farmland; (2) land conservation and tenure; (3) land use, agricultural production, and farm income; and (4) additional considerations.

Price, Size, and Availability of Farmland

The heart of this issue is whether foreign investment prevents (presumably young) would-be domestic farmers from entering that occupation. Such might be the case for one (or both) of two reasons. First, in an everything else being equal framework, the presence of foreigners as net demanders of farmland shifts the total demand for farmland outward, driving up equilibrium prices for farmland (see figure 3–1). The domestic supply-demand

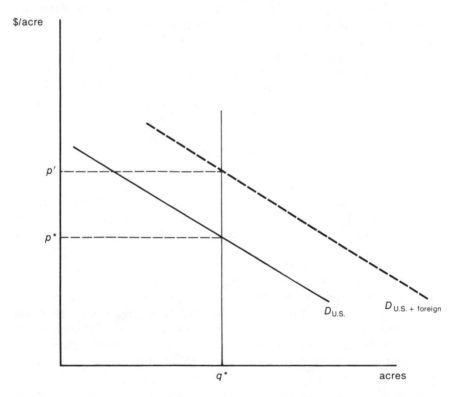

Figure 3–1. The Impact of Foreign Demand for U.S. Farmland on Per-
Acre Farmland Prices

equilibrium of farmland changing hands occurs with a quantity $q*$ being exchanged at a per-acre price $p*$. The inclusion of a foreign component in the market for agricultural land shifts out the demand curve from D to D', and, while the quantity of farmland exchanged does not vary, equilibrium price per acre rises to p'. This, of course, tells us nothing about the age distribution of the buyers.

It is often argued, however, that foreign investors pay high (read "above-market") prices for agricultural land. If this is so, then creation of a capital barrier to entry for young U.S. farmers would be a credible argument against foreign ownership of U.S. farmland.[9] The facts are not very supportive of this thesis. Jansma, et al. (1981), conclude that, in comparison with the total market, the foreign investment component is so small that the overall impact of foreign investment on prices paid for farmland by domestic farmers is minimal. USDA investigation of the relationship between foreign investment and land-price inflation has uncovered no systematic patterns: rates of land-price increase are found to be related positively to the rate of purchase by foreigners in some states and related negatively in other states.[10]

The driving force behind the land-price increases of the 1960s and 1970s was not the foreign presence, but rather farmland expansion *by existing farmers.* The foreign component of the demand for farmland contributed marginally at best to the farmland price inflation over this period.

With respect to farm leases the story is no different. Were it the case that foreign owners charged higher rents on their farms, blocking this form of entry into farming for young U.S. farmers, one would again have a valid economic rationale for regulation. The facts do not support this hypothesis either. Most foreign investors in fact lease the land back to local farmers, and the crop-sharing or cash leasing arrangements do not differ in any significant respects from those assigned by domestic farmer/landlords (Currie, et al. 1976; USDA 1980).

Jansma, et al. (1981) highlight an additional consideration vis-à-vis the so-called problem of foreigners bidding up the price of farmland—namely, higher prices are only a problem from the standpoint of excluded buyers. The sellers, however, have presumably received a payment sufficient to overwhelm any opportunity costs of keeping the land, and the sale has made them better off. Since the sellers are usually members of the farming community, the net impact of foreign investment on higher farmland prices (were it true) is uncertain. Given the redistribution-of-wealth considerations, it would, clearly, be somewhat less than accurate to ignore the supply side of the equation.

The second way in which foreign investment might preclude entrance into farming concerns the impact of such investment on the size and number of farms. The steady increase in farm size and decrease in numbers of farms has, of course, been well chronicled by investigators (see chapter 2). To the extent that foreign participation in the U.S. agricultural sector contributes in a significant fashion to required acreage expansion over time, there would again be a barrier-to-entry argument against foreign ownership of farmland, since, all else being equal, an increasing acreage requirement raises the capital requirements for entry into farming as an occupation. The specific issue of causality raised here can be addressed by answering two related questions: why average acreage farmed is increasing over time, and to what extent the changing structure of agriculture in this respect is the result of foreign investment in U.S. farmland.

There is strong evidence to suggest that economies of size are responsible, in large measure, for the steady increase in average farm size over the twentieth century. Technological advances in agricultural science have continually raised the acreage required to capture all relevant economies of scale in production.[11] Expansion is required in order to remain competitive; yet, obviously, not everyone can expand. This outward shifting of the demand-for-farmland curve created a severe upward pressure on per-acre prices at about the same time as foreign investment in U.S. farmland started receiving popular attention. Even though the two events are associated, the relationship is not causal in nature. Structural changes in agricultural production that were already underway in the 1940s and 1950s played a major role in the farmland price inflation of the 1960s and 1970s. Indeed, during this period of time, farm expansion was the primary motive listed by two-thirds of farmland purchasers.[12]

The impact of foreign investment on farm size is really a question of the magnitude of the foreign investment activity and the types (acreage) of farm units being purchased. There are several reasons why larger tracts would appeal to the foreign investor. Jansma, et al. (1981) list four: (1) the fact that normally higher transaction costs (including avoiding disclosure laws) incurred by foreigners can be spread over more acres; (2) a general preference by foreign owners for crop (as opposed to livestock) operations; (3) the reliance by most foreign investors on professional managers; and (4) the ease of purchasing complete farming operations in comparison with so-called add-on acreage. Of course, for a variety of other marketing reasons, price per acre usually falls as the size of the tract to be exchanged increases, all else the same.

It is generally true that foreigners tend to purchase farm units of greater acreage than the average for the type of farm operation contemplated. However, purchase of one tract consisting of fifteen hundred acres is substantively different (to the foreign buyer) from purchase of five three-hundred-acre tracts that can be combined into one farm. Purchase behavior of the latter sort would reduce the total number of small farms that might qualify as entry-level farms to potential newcomers, significantly altering the overall structure of the farmland real estate market. The potential barrier to entry by young U.S. farmers is obvious. Again, however, the pattern of purchases by foreigners tends toward purchase of larger tracts, and calls into question the fundamental link between foreign investment and negative impacts on domestic farmers in this respect.

Land Conservation and Tenure

Foreigners do not appear to be taking agricultural land out of production. This is the unanimous finding by researchers into the implications of foreign investment for land tenure arrangements.

Section V of the Agricultural Foreign Investment Disclosure Act (1978) requires the USDA to determine the impacts of foreign ownership of U.S. agricultural land, especially the effects on family farms and rural communities. Results of USDA reports filed with the U.S. Congress under this mandate are reported in table 3–1.

In terms of intended use, foreign buyers of U.S. farmland rarely differ from the before-purchase operational use. The largest percentage of foreign owners responding to USDA queries about tenure also indicate retention of current management and/or lease arrangements. For the four-year period for which these data are currently available, these categories show a high degree of stability as well.

A high rate of tenancy (that is, high turnover of managers or tenant farmers) is widely regarded as antithetical to the rural farm community. The argument is that tenant farmers (and their families) are less likely to develop an interest (and thus participate) in the life of the local farm community and economy. There does appear to be some evidence that suggests that absentee

Table 3–1
Impacts of Foreign Ownership on Use of Farmland and Tenure[a]
(*percentages*)

Date	No Change in Intended Use	No Change in Tenure	Some Change in Tenure	No Reply
Feb. 1979–Dec. 1980	89	45	37	18
1981	92	42	27	31
1982	92	42	29	29

Source: USDA, Economics and Statistics Service, *Foreign Ownership of U.S. Agricultural Land,* Agriculture Information Bulletin 448 (February 1979–December 1980); and USDA, Economic Research Service, *Foreign Ownership of U.S. Agricultural Land* (through December 31, 1981) and (through December 31, 1982).

[a]Responses measured as a percentage of total acreage.

owners are less prone than owner-operators to involve themselves in civic projects (Rodefeld 1979; Jansma, et al. 1981). Despite the obvious incentives for managers and tenants to freeload on civic efforts undertaken by local residents, there remains no documented evidence of significant differences between foreign-owned and domestically owned tenancy arrangements in terms of tenant involvement in the local community.

A related issue concerns the incentives facing tenants, and foreign owners in particular, with respect to conservation and land improvement programs. The implicit assumption that underlies this question is that foreign owners, for a variety of reasons (such as differing rates of time preference or the manner in which they view their investments) have less incentive than do their domestic counterparts to maintain or upgrade the quality of the farming operation, with obvious consequences for the long-run health of the land.

No doubt, the shorter effective planning horizon for tenant farmers does reduce their incentive to undertake costly capital programs in the areas of conservation or land improvement. Jansma, et al. (1981) cite a study by Johnson (1974) in which the author finds that 90 percent of the leases in two selected regions of Michigan and Illinois are for one-year terms, and that two-thirds of the leases are verbal in nature. Nevertheless, lease renewals prevail to the extent that *effective* length of lease averaged eleven years in Michigan and fourteen years in Illinois.

The critical issue, again, is whether these suggested shirking incentives exist to a greater extent for the foreign owner than for the domestic farmer-renter. Given the presumption that both foreign and domestic farm owners seek to maximize their long-run return on investment, there should exist no differential motive for domestic farmers to undertake capital improvements while foreign owners allow their land to languish. The study by Lassey, et al. (1978) sheds some empirical light on the issue. Focusing on the specific conservation practice of erosion control in the state of Washington, the authors find that soil erosion is perceived as a more significant problem by domestic farm owners than by foreign owners. In addition, however, they report that greater support for erosion control exists among foreign owners than among domestic farmers. The findings of this study obviously do not support the proposition that there is a negative relationship between nonresident alien (NRA) ownership of U.S. farmland and the level of conservation efforts.

Land Use: The Intensity Question

Does foreign ownership of U.S. farmland influence the manner in which that land is utilized? How do land-use decisions of foreign-owned farms affect subsequent farm production and income? Jansma, et al. (1981) present considerations that bear on the issue of the intensity of use of the farmland resource by foreigners.[13]

First, they recognize that returns to the labor input in farming may be differentially valued by domestic, family farmers and absentee owners. This latter category would clearly include foreign owners. If this argument is correct, one is led to the conclusion that foreigners will farm their acreage less intensively than domestic farm owners. There are several problems with this reasoning. If it is true that domestic and foreign owners subjectively value the labor resource differently (in the directions indicated previously), then, according to standard economic investment theory, this will be reflected in differing mixes between labor and capital employed by members of the two groups, but it tells us nothing about intensity of the farming effort. What is suggested, however, is that for any given level of land-use intensity, domestic farmers will be prone to favor a higher labor/capital mix and foreigners will favor a lower labor/capital mix. Evidence on the relative sizes of farm tracts purchased by foreigners is supportive of this argument—foreigners tend to purchase tracts that are larger on average than those purchased by domestic buyers. This is to be expected if foreigners are attempting to purchase sufficient acreage to ensure complete capture of relevant economies of scale related to their higher capital/labor ratio. The fact that foreign investors are less able to control the agency problem with their managers and/or tenants should also drive foreigners to favor a high capital/labor ratio, and tells us nothing about intensity of farmland use between foreign-owned and domestically owned farms.

The second possibility raised in the Jansma study is that foreign investors might engage in more intensive use of the farmland resource; a result of shorter time horizons than their U.S. counterparts. Essentially, the argument is that foreigners, in search of a higher nominal return on their investment than domestic family farmers, farm the land extremely intensively for several years, exploiting the productive capabilities of the soil, then resell the tract. Of course, by the time of sale, soil fertility would be exhausted, which should, in turn, be capitalized into the sales price of the farm, assuming it is not costly for potential buyers to acquire information about the land they are interested in. Presumably, foreign investors balance off these two considerations in their wealth-maximation strategies. This issue of intensity of use remains an empirical one and awaits the rigorous testing that has not been accomplished thus far.

Additional Considerations

Wealth redistribution considerations affect the question of the desirability of foreign ownership of U.S. farmland. It was indicated previously that even if foreign investors were willing to pay above-market prices for U.S. farmland, beneficiaries of such a plan would in fact include those farmers who were net sellers of farmland. Similarly, public policy with respect to acreage allotments and price supports may impart sizable capital gains to foreign owners, who probably free-ride on lobbying efforts of domestic farmers to obtain these protections. These capital gains include higher earnings on the crops cultivated, as well as higher capitalized values of the land itself.[14]

The wealth gains accruing to the foreign investor as a consequence of these public policies may be sizable. Maier, et al. (1960) found per-acre gains in capitalized value of land under tobacco allotments in 1957 that varied from $1,600 to $2,500.[15] To the extent that domestic, family farmers (and hence, policymakers) view such wealth gains by foreigners as undesirable, then some regulatory activity may be justified *in a distributive sense,* even though it fails to meet the established criteria for economic efficiency.

A second consideration in determining the net impact of foreign investment in U.S. farmland is the potential response by respective foreign countries to successful regulatory efforts by the U.S. state governments against foreign investors.[16] Given the relative significance of U.S. investment overseas (book value of U.S. investments abroad is roughly four times the value of foreign investments in the United States[17]), the potential adverse net impact of regulation warrants consideration in the decision-making calculus of elected officials. Again, however, special-interests jockeying via the political process for wealth redistribution in their favor may value this impact very high or very low, according to their own position.

A third consideration concerns the impact on a highly valued agrarian ideal. Family farming is viewed as not only a specific form of business organization, but also as a way of life. Sales of U.S. agricultural land may threaten this concept of farming (as an ideal) and impose negative externalities on the society as a whole. The value of this ideal should not be underestimated. In state after state, reference is made to the threat, real or imagined, that foreign investment poses to the continued existence and stability of the family farm unit. These references show up in the introductory statements to legislative measures that seek to impose restrictions on foreign ownership of U.S. farmland, or in accompanying statements provided by the bills' sponsors. For example, Section 1 of California Assembly Bill number 263, introduced January 11, 1979, and of Pennsylvania House Bill number 853, introduced March 27, 1979, read as follows.

> The legislature further declares that the wise use of land is best encouraged through land ownership such as through a farm system composed primarily by family farmers; that foreign, absentee ownership is detrimental to such purposes; and that foreign investment in California (Pennsylvania) agricultural land tends to increase speculation and exploitation of agricultural

land and products, thereby causing higher prices to consumers of agricultural products, greater instability of market conditions, and the further decline of family farming and wise rural development in this state.

A fourth factor to consider is the passivity (or lack thereof) of the actors themselves. As Loveman (1976) points out, U.S. firms investing abroad have a long history of attempting, with some degree of success, to influence political outcomes in the countries in which they have an interest.[18] Similarly, he argues, foreign investors in U.S. real estate (or other types of investment) may have incentives to become involved in the U.S. political and/or legal process, at the local, state, and national levels, in order to influence legislative outcomes with respect to land-use policy. There is a circularity problem inherent in this facet of the structure of U.S. agriculture that cannot be ignored, and which requires sophisticated empirical testing of differences in land use by foreign and domestic owners.

Finally, as suggested by Goffney (1976), the cost of implementing a program design to regulate foreign investment in U.S. farm real estate qualifies as a legitimate impact of foreign investment. Even if, as is generally the case, the burden of reporting falls on the foreign investor, there are substantial administrative costs borne by agencies charged with the task of monitoring and/or enforcing restrictions on foreign ownership of U.S. farmland. USDA costs for administering the AFIDA disclosure requirements are detailed in table 3-2. These costs understate by a considerable amount the true costs of administration and enforcement, since they do not include aggregate totals for the state agencies in states with similar reporting requirements or o᠁ nership restrictions.

Macroeconomic Impacts

Foreign investors in U.S. farmland may create external (spillover) costs that affect the local economic community in which the farm is located. That is,

Table 3–2
USDA Costs of Administering the AFIDA Regulations and Fines Collected

Year	Administration Costs	Late Filing Penalties Assessed
1979	$600,000	—
1980	$509,000	$250,000
1981	$530,500	$535,000
1982	$362,000	$416,000

Source: USDA, Economics and Statistics Service, *Foreign Ownership of U.S. Agricultural Land* (February 1979–December 1980); and USDA, Economic Research Service, *Foreign Ownership of U.S. Agricultural Land* (through December 31, 1981) and (through December 31, 1982).

actions undertaken by the foreign, absentee owner may affect the performance of the local, economic community. As noted by Jansma, et al. (1981), care must be taken by the principal investigators of impact studies to separate structural changes in the industry of agriculture itself from changes wrought in a rural community by the phenomenon in question.[19] That is to say, foreign investors may exert two types of influence on the community: direct effects and indirect effects (that occur because the entire structure of agriculture changes). Any indirect effects must, of course, be separated out from other structural changes that may be concurrent but unrelated, in any causal fashion, to the presence of foreigners in the domestic farmland market. The problem for the researcher attempting to empirically measure the impact of foreign investment on rural communities is that, until recently, the magnitude of the foreign presence was undocumented, and associated structural changes were not apparent. Still, according to Jansma, et al. (1981), the combination of a conceptual framework for evaluating the economic impact of foreign investment on local communities, information from existing impact studies, and available data on the incidence of foreign ownership of U.S. farmland is enough to permit (1) advancement of hypotheses concerning the manner in which rural communities are affected by foreign investment, and (2) identification of additional information required for assigning correct estimates of impacts under study.[20]

In the last half of their study, Jansma, et al. (1981) identify five areas of concern to be addressed in any discussion of the macroeconomic impacts of foreign investment on the surrounding community: (1) measurement issues associated with intensity of use; (2) spatial purchasing patterns; (3) nonlocal marketing; (4) fiscal impacts on local governments; and (5) complexity of economic structures. To these five must be added a sixth area, not of concern, but of relevant interest in the macroeconomic and microeconomic sense: the potential economic impacts of forbidding or otherwise restricting foreign investment in U.S. farmland.

Intensity of Land Use

As was noted briefly earlier, the operational decisions made by a specific farmer will spill over to influence economic activity in the surrounding economic community. Type of crop, intensity of land use, associated capital/labor ratio employed in production, and other aspects of the farming operation influence the volume of goods and services exported from and imported into the local community, and thus, the general level of economic activity. Since agricultural products are a significant portion of the exports in rural areas of the country, patterns of foreign ownership of U.S. farmland that imply differential intensity of land use would also imply potentially greater or lesser economic activity within the local rural community, depending on the direction of the intensity effect. Several authors have suggested that, in fact, foreign owners farm the land *less* intensively than their U.S.-citizen neighbors, even if patterns of crop cultivation do not differ significantly between the two groups.[21]

The conceptual arguments are contradictory, however. Goffney (1976, pp. 147–63) reasons that foreigners who purchase farmland for security-of-investment reasons may not conduct their farming operations in a profit-maximizing fashion. In the same volume, Dovring (pp. 132–46) argues that foreigners attempt to maximize net income from renting their farms instead of maximizing net value of production. Both arguments imply that foreign owners farm their land less intensively than domestic farmers, with predictable consequences for the level of exports and economic activity more generally, within the surrounding farm community. On the other hand, Jansma, et al. (1981, p. 4) suggest that foreign owners of U.S. farmland may have a shorter time horizon than U.S. farmers, which motivates them to exploit the natural fertility of the land to a greater degree than domestic farmers. Their argument implies just the opposite of the ones by Goffney and Dovring. Increased exploitation suggests a higher level of both exports and imports, and thus greater prosperity for the surrounding community, at least in the short run.

If the conceptual issues are contradictory, the results of empirical investigations are not. The USDA findings reported in table 3-1 show no evidence that intended land use by foreign buyers is significantly different from the previous owners'. There is no reported differential regarding intensity of land use between foreign and domestic owners of U.S. farmland in the Iowa State study, conducted for the USDA.[22] The Penn State (Jansma) study also finds no empirical proof of an intensity-of-use dispartiy favoring U.S. owner-operators over NRAs. To the contrary, Jansma, et al. (1981, p. 18) found that intensity of farm effort actually increased with foreign ownership in eight of the twenty-four counties they surveyed, and decreased in only one county.

Spatial Purchasing Patterns

The spatial purchasing patterns of foreign investors are of concern to investigators of the impact of such investment on the local community. At issue is the supposed tendency for foreign owners to behave differently than U.S. farmers with respect to purchase of production inputs and economic rents.

It has been argued that foreign owners will tend to purchase inputs into the farm production process (such as machinery, fertilizers, and seed) large, primarily regional, sellers, rather than from local, retail outlets.[23] To the extent that the behavior of foreign landowners differs, in this respect, from that of domestic farmers, there would be a negative impact on the economic prosperity of the local community. The differential propensity for nonresident or resident aliens to purchase nonlabor inputs from large, regional outlets, or from the manufacturers themselves, has not, to my knowledge, ever been determined empirically. However, as Jansma, et al. (1981) point out, a large majority of foreign investors in U.S. farmland are absentee owners whose interests lie in the security (monetary and political) of the investment. Management responsibilities are generally contracted out to local farmers, whose input-purchase decisions probably differ little from those of their neighbors. With this in mind, it is clear that in most respects the spatial purchasing patterns of foreign owners with respect to labor inputs are also little different from their domestic neighbors.

In two respects, however, there may be differences. Any economic rents accruing to the U.S. farmer remain within the local farm community (as consumption expenditures, capital improvements on the land, savings at the local financial institution, and so on) for the most part, whereas the foreign owner may take part or all of the net profits out of the specific farm locale, and perhaps out of the United States completely. Two factors tend to minimize the impact of this differential spatial pattern of spending. First, of course, is the well-documented, minute incidence of foreign ownership of U.S. farmland. Second, accounting profits will probably be lower for the foreign, absentee owner than for the domestic, owner-operator. The foreigner must contract and pay for labor and managerial services; costs that are deducted from revenues in the accounting statement. Owner-operators is less likely to charge themselves for both labor and managerial services. Any attempted estimation of the net outflow of profits must be based on profits earned by foreign-owned, manager-operated farms, not average reported profits on all farms.

The fact that foreign purchasers tend to prefer positions of higher equity than do U.S. farmers, and obtain mortgage funds from outside (nonlocal) sources, also implies that local communities may suffer adverse consequences as a result of foreign investment, relative to comparable investment by local farmers. Local sources of loanable funds would not be patronized by foreigners to the same extent as they would be domestic farmers.

USDA reports, filed under requirements of the Agricultural Foreign Investment Disclosure Act (1978), indicate that a large percentage of foreign buyers pay cash for their farmland purchases. Forty-six percent of all foreign-owned parcels identified by the USDA in their 1981 report were purchased entirely by cash.[24] Over the subsequent year (January 1 to December 31, 1982), cash sales constituted 57 percent of the foreign purchases of U.S. farmland.[25]

Nonlocal Marketing

Concern over nonlocal marketing of their produce by foreign owners is twofold. First, it has been suggested that foreigners may ship their products directly out of the country, bypassing local shippers—to the obvious detriment of the local economy. Jansma, et al. (1981) predict the net effect of such shipments to be negligible, however.[26] Indeed, there are no estimates of the differential extent to which foreigners engage in direct export of their agricultural produce. Second, foreign owners may deal with regional, instead of local, shippers to a greater extent than domestic farmers. The evidence provided by the Iowa State study (see note 23) on this aspect of foreign ownership is inconclusive. In two of the three states examined, the proportion of foreign-owned tracts from which crops were sold to regional outlets rather than local outlets did not vary significantly from the proportion of domestically owned tracts. In comparison to U.S.-citizen-owned farms that were rented out in Iowa, foreigners were found to utilize regional shippers to a significantly greater degree than local shippers.[27]

Fiscal Impacts

Net revenues and expenditures of local governments are likely to be affected little if at all by foreign investment in U.S. farmland. The minute incidence of participation by foreigners in the domestic farmland market renders conceptual effects insignificant.

   With respect to the receipts side of the balance sheet, foreign investment, insofar as it contributes to a rise in the assessed value of agricultural land, may benefit local governments. That is to say, total tax revenues would rise without a corresponding increase in the tax rate, if foreign investment was responsible for driving up farmland prices. To the extent that foreign owners have a propensity to invest in improving the land itself (with irrigation, buildings, and so on) to a greater degree than domestic farmers, coffers of the local governments, which rely heavily on the property tax for revenues, will fill all the faster. If foreign investment had the net effect of stimulating the local economy, the ultimate effect would be to increase the relevant tax base of the local jurisdiction. Since the large majority of foreign-owned farms are leased or managed by U.S. farmers whose production behavior is similar, in most respects, to domestic owner-operators, these suggested effects are likely to be negligible.

   Demands by foreign owners for community-based services are also likely to be insignificant. Direct demand for services such as schooling is nonexistent among absentee owners. Other services (such as police and fire protection and road paving) may be available (if needed) to the foreign owner on a more or less pro-rata basis. Indirect demand for community services might be generated by foreign owners whose net impact was to increase the general level of economic activity within the local community. By and large, the net effects will be small, and probably positive

The distributive aspect of this issue deserves brief mention at this point. To the extent that foreign, especially absentee, owners support the local community (via property taxes) without taking back a proportional share of the community's expenditures on services, local inhabitants receive a net transfer of wealth in the form of lower taxes. Farm managers may also receive a rent transfer of this type, in the sense that their children may utilize the local school system which is paid for by taxes levied on their employers. Unless these effects are capitalized correctly into the prevailing wage structure for managers, they also are recipients of a net wealth transfer from foreign owners.

Complexity of Economic Structures

Jansma, et al. (1981) discuss the potential impact of foreign investment on the complexity of economic structure, particularly the availability of investment capital in rural areas, at some length. They suggest that foreign investment in U.S. agricultural land will increase the supply of investment capital in rural communities, since local farmers, as sellers, tend to deposit sales proceeds in local financial institutions.[28] Benefits to the entire community can be expected to result from this type of capital flow. Farmers and other local entrepreneurs may have investment opportunities that require issuance of loan capital before those opportunities can be exploited. If the inflow of foreign capital raises the supply of capital available in the associated rural community, the economic consequences may be significant. Increased investment by farmers might mean increased purchases of inputs from local businesses, and greater crop productivity, which would ultimately result in an increased volume of agricultural exports from the community. Similarly, comparable investment by members of the nonfarm business community might create spillover demands for the produce from local farmers. In both cases, increased local investment serves to stimulate the local economy, in terms of employment and income, which, in turn, boosts available revenue sources to the local government.

**Potential Economic Impacts of Restricting
Foreign Ownership of U.S. Farmland**

Although the economic impact of foreign investment on farmers and rural communities is a legitimate concern of policymakers, it does not embody the economist's concept of opportunity cost as well as might be hoped. For purposes of evaluating a public policy of prohibiting nonresident alien ownership of U.S. farmland, economic impacts of foreign investment, per se, while relevant, do not constitute a comprehensive review of the economic costs and benefits of the public policy. Additional information is needed: actual and opportunity costs connected with implementing public policy itself must be considered. Table 3-2 reported administration costs incurred by the USDA in complying with the AFIDA reporting requirements. In a macroeconomic setting, the associated costs are net opportunity costs.

Removal of ownership of U.S. farmland as an investment alternative to foreigners has consequences for the pattern of foreign investment in the United States. Removal of one of the portfolio options available to foreigners will result in shifts toward other types of investments (a normal substitution effect). The nature of substitute investment patterns will determine, in conjunction with the suggested microeconomic and macroeconomic impacts discussed previously, the net impact of public policies designed to restrict or prohibit foreign investment in U.S. farmland.

The obvious alternative investment available to foreigners is urban real estate. But what types of urban real estate will the foreign investor tend to favor? In what ways might family farmers and rural communities be affected by these new patterns of investment? Impacts could potentially be significant, especially if foreign attention focused of investment in the so-called urban fringe. The empirical lacuna with respect to this aspect of public policy formation on the foreign investment issue is severe.

The shift of funds from the rural to the urban setting has predictable consequences for the supply of investment funds in rural areas—namely, it will decline, as will the economic well-being of the local farm communities. Such a shift could also alter the basic structure of agriculture in two respects: foreign investment might increase in one or more of the processing or marketing stages of agriculture, and foreign investment might create a shift in the pattern of demand for agricultural products. More information on this aspect of the impact of a public policy that restricts foreign investment would permit more comprehensive evaluation of the relevant costs and benefits of pursuing such a policy.

Concluding Comments

If the general tone of the preceding discussion tended to downplay the recognized economic impact of foreign investment in U.S. farmland on family farmers and local farm communities, there is good reason: on the basis of existing information, economic impacts of such investment by nonresident aliens on members of the farming community are negligible. In this respect, the conclusions put forth in this chapter are no different from the conclusions of the Jansma, et al. (1981) study, or the USDA observations in their AFIDA reports of 1980, 1981, and 1982. Foreign owners of U.S. agricultural land tend to either rent the land back to local farmers or hire local farmers as managers. Both courses of action imply no significant change in farm-use strategy, at either the production or distribution levels. Even if the proposed impacts discussed earlier were valid, the tiny magnitude of foreign ownership of farm real estate renders any hypothesized effect insignificant.

This leaves us, of course, in an awkward position. The evidence seems clearly enough to refute the proposition that foreign investment imposes significant negative externalities. It seem pointless to even issue the standard call for more research. Yet half of the state governments in the United States have imposed legislative restrictions on nonresident alien ownership of U.S. farmland. This presents us with the seeming contradiction that while investigators can find no empirically valid harm from foreign ownership of U.S. farmland, regulation is a fact of life in virtually all of the midwestern farm states. In Chapter 4 I shall attempt to escape from this dilemma.

Notes

1. There may, admittedly, be other types of consequences of foreign investment in U.S. farmland—social and/or political. Since I am concerned with isolating an economic motive for regulation, I focus exclusively upon the economic impacts of foreign ownership of U.S. agricultural land.

2. J.D. Jansma, F. Goode, K. Gertel, and P. Small, *Implications of Foreign Ownership of U.S. Farmland on Farms and Rural Communities* Bulletin 832 (Pennsylvania State University, January 1981): 32 pp.

3. In 1981, for example, nonresident aliens sold 325 tracts of land with an aggregate of 272,910 acres. See USDA, *Foreign Ownership of U.S. Agricultural Land: through December 31, 1982,* p. 49.

4. A ground-living fungus, for example, could destroy crops on many neighboring farms, as could contaminated water.

5. J.P. Friedman, "The Real Estate Industry and the Foreign Investor," in *Monitoring Foreign Ownership of U.S. Real Estate,* vol. 1, USDA (1979):12–57.

6. Friedman (see note 5, p. 54) identifies time lags in updating assessment rolls, lack of thoroughness of tax appraisals, and desire of local jurisdictions to show low values in order to receive more state support as three reasons why assessed values understate fair market value.

7. See G.W. Heineman, "Pursuing the Foreign Investor," *Real Estate Review* vol. 10, no. 2 (Summer 1980):44–47; and General Accounting Of-

Office, *Foreign Ownership of U.S. Land: Much Concern, Little Data,* Report of the Comptroller General of the United States (June 1978).

8. USDA, Economic Research Service, *Foreign Ownership of U.S. Agricultural Land: through December 31, 1982.,* p. vii.

9. Jansma, et al. (see note 2).

10. The oft-cited tax advantages enjoyed by foreigners that enable them to outbid American citizens for farmland is an irrelevant side issue. From the perspective of evaluating economic impact, the fact that foreigners have more money to spend is the relevant consideration, not why they have more money.

11. See *Foreign Ownership of U.S. Agricultural Land,* USDA, No. 447 (February 1980); and Y. Lu, "Technological Change and Structure," in *Structure Issues in American Agriculture* USDA, No. 438 (May 1979).

12. *Foreign Investment in the United States,* Practicing Law Institute (Series No. 297, 1979):352.

13. Jansma, et al. (see note 2), p. 5.

14. See, for example, J.B. Bullock, W.L. Nienwondt, and E.C. Pasour, Jr., "Land Values and Allotment Rents," *American Journal of Agricultural Economics,* vol. 59 (1977):380–84.

15. F. Maier, J. Hendricks, and W.L. Gibson, Jr., *The Sale of Flue-Cured Tobacco Allotments,* Virginia Polytechnic Institute, Agricultural Experiment Station, Bulletin 148 (1960).

16. This issue is raised by (among others) W. Fletcher and K. Cook, "Foreign Investment in U.S. Farmland: An Overview," *Foreign Investment in United States Agricultural Land* (Washington, D.C.: Committee on Agriculture, Nutrition and Forestry, 95th Congress, 2nd Session—1979): 3–21; and Legislative Staff Report, *Nonresident Alien Ownership of Agricultural Lands in Florida,* Senate Committee on Agriculture and House Committee on Agriculture and General legislation (February 11, 1980):27.

17. *Agriculture Census Guide,* for the 1978 Census of Agriculture, U.S. Department of Commerce (1978).

18. B. Loveman, "Political Implications of Foreign Investment in Land in the United States," in *Foreign Investment in U.S. Real Estate,* vol. 1, USDA (1979):12–57.

19. Jansma, et al. (see note 2), p. 16.

20. Ibid.

21. See, for example, M. Gaffney, "Social and Economic Impacts of Foreign Investment in U.S. Land," in *Foreign Investment in U.S. Real Estate, USDA,* (1976):147–63; F. Dovring, "Economic Impact of Foreign Investment in Real Estate," in *Foreign Investment in U.S. Real Estate* (pp. 132–46); and P.W. Barkley and L.F. Rogers, "Problems Associated with Foreign Ownership of U.S. Farmland," in *Foreign Investment in United States Agricultural Land* (see note 16), pp. 22–36.

22. General results of this study are reported in USDA, *Foreign Ownership of U.S. Agricultural Land: through December 31, 1981* (1982):56–57.

23. See especially, I.W. Schmedemann, "Foreign Investment in Rural Land of Texas and the Southewest," in *Foreign Investment in U.S. Real Estate* (see note 21), 111–123; and J.H. Atkinson and B.F. Jones, "Should Foreigners Own Our Land?" *Foreign Investment in United States Agricultural Land* (see note 16), pp. 57–62.

24. USDA (see note 3), p. 22.

25. USDA (see note 8), p. 43.

26. Jansma, et al., (see note 2), p. 20.

27. USDA (see note 22), pp. 56–57.

28. Jansma, et al., (see note 2), pp. 22.

4 The Demand for Regulation

Cultivators of the earth are the most valuable citizens, the most vigorous, the most independent, the most virtuous. They are tied to their country and wedded to its liberty and interests by the most lasting bonds.

—Thomas Jefferson

Over the course of its development, the United States has been the repository of many billions of dollars worth of investment by foreigners. This investment has generally been relatively unimpeded, and, in many instances, individual states have encouraged foreign investment. In the 1970s, however, foreign direct investment in the United States, particularly investment by nonresident aliens (NRAs) in U.S. farmland, became the focus of considerable attention, indignation, inspection, and, ultimately, regulation.

To many economists, the indignation and regulation appear at first, and even at second glance, irrational. It is well known that an efficient economic order requires that resources be allocated to their most highly valued uses without regard to who owns the resulting property rights. Yet the facts remain: along with the flood of purchases of U.S. real estate by NRAs in the 1970s, relative to previous years, an avalanche of state and national regulations applying to NRA ownership of farmland appeared. Where regulation had not occurred as of mid-1981, lack of effort in the state legislatures was not the reason; restrictions had been proposed in forty-one states.

Further questioning of the rationality of regulation serves no purpose, save to divert attention away from important issues. Since regulation is now an accomplished fact, we must assume that some group(s) had legitimate reasons for seeking the aid of the state in achieving it. The questions that remain are (1) who demanded the restrictions on foreign participation in the domestic farmland market; (2) why did they do so; and (3) what factors determine the prevailing pattern of legal restrictions against NRA ownership of farmland?

The regulation of farmland can be analyzed within the usual supply-demand framework of standard economic analysis. The first two questions cut to the heart of the demand side of the equation. The latter question is directed at determining the supply side of the equation. Together they provide a forceful explanation of the pattern of regulation. State legal restrictions against foreigners are explored more fully in chapter 6.

Features of the Regulatory Process

There are two peculiar features of the regulatory process in regard to foreign ownership of farmland. First, public concern has focused on foreign investment in agricultural land, particularly that which lies in relatively small farm units and in patterns of ownership referred to as family farms. This is despite the fact that foreign investment in U.S. farmland represents only a fraction of all foreign investment in this country. As of 1979, for example, real estate comprised only about 5 percent of the more than $40 billion of direct investment held by NRAs in the United States.[1] Less than 1 percent of this investment was in private farmland.[2] For the eighteen-month period from January 1, 1977 through June 30, 1978, sales of farmland to NRA investors amounted to about eight one-hundredths (0.08) of one percent of all U.S. farmland. Even though foreign investment in such urban real estate as shopping centers, office buildings, and other commercial property is far greater in value than investment in rural, particularly farm, real estate, public concern has focused clearly on farmland.

Second, farm lobby groups constitute the only identifiable private interests backing the proposed restrictions against foreigners. I conducted a survey in 1981 and found that the only interest groups offering legislation designed to restrict foreign ownership of U.S. farmland were lobbying organizations maintained by farm and agricultural interests.[3] These organizations are extremely effective. As of mid-1979, fifteen states had enacted legislation that placed major acreage or other restraints on ownership of farmland by NRAs (see table 4-1). Moreover, at the time of the survey, several other state legislatures had considered or were considering passage of similar restraints.

The Politics of Redistribution

The restrictions chronicled in table 4-1 have the effect of redistributing income away from potential foreign owners of U.S. farmland to domestic farmers. No doubt this helps motivate the underlying demand for regulation. But the impact on domestic farmers of regulating foreign investment in U.S. farmland is much greater than that on net. The remainder of this chapter will investigate the family farmer's economic interest in regulation. I assume that farmers desire to maximize the net value of their capital at all points in time. This capital has two components: the farmland and other physical assets such as the buildings and machinery, and the farmer's knowledge and skill, or *human capital*.[4]

The argument is that those owners of farmland who desire to maximize their net wealth are net demanders of farmland, and, as a consequence, such owners of small farms are desirous of relatively lower prices for land.

Table 4–1
Major State Restrictions of Foreign Ownership of Farmland

State	Restriction
Arkansas	NRA[a] ownership not allowed
Connecticut	NRA ownership not allowed
Illinois	NRA must dispose of holdings within 6 years
Indiana	320-acre limit for NRAs
Iowa	NRA ownership not allowed
Kentucky	NRA must dispose of holdings within 8 years
Minnesota	NRA ownership not allowed
Mississippi	NRA ownership not allowed
Missouri	5-acre limit for NRAs
Nebraska	NRA ownership not allowed
North Dakota	NRA ownership not allowed
Oklahoma	NRA ownership not allowed
Pennsylvania	5,000-acre limit for NRAs
South Dakota	160-acre limit for NRAs
Wisconsin	640-acre limit for NRAs

Source: *Monitoring Foreign Ownership of U.S. Real Estate*, Report to Congress vol. 1 (USDA, 1979), pp. 61–92.
[a]NRA = nonresident alien.

In typically rational economic fashion, owners of small farms—primarily the so-called family farmers—will attempt to depress land prices via the political process (as one of their several alternatives) so long as the benefits, measured in relative terms as lower prices of land, exceed the costs of actions required to obtain the benefits.

When the sale of U.S. farmland to nonresident aliens is evaluated from an *efficiency* standpoint, some economists would conclude that there should be no restrictions on NRAs owning U.S. land devoted to farming (or any other kind of use) and that farmers have nothing to complain about. However, as public-choice theorists have demonstrated repeatedly, and as actions undertaken by family farmers demonstrate, much real-world behavior is devoted to attempts to influence the distribution, rather than the size, of the economic pie. Individuals or groups will attempt (by threat postures, data gathering, information distortion, and the political process) to influence terms of trade until the expected benefits from seeking to influence the distribution of the pie equal the costs of engaging in such activity.

A theory that explains the pattern of legislative action restricting ownership of U.S. farmland by NRAs must provide reasonable explanations for the following questions.

1. Why do restraints result from the miniscule incidence of NRA participation in the domestic farmland market?
2. Why are restraints imposed on NRAs only?
3. Why are restraints targeted specifically at NRA investment in domestic farmland and not at NRA investment in other real estate or business?

Farmers, Technology, and the Demand for Farmland

The basic issue raised by the first question just listed concerns the rationality farmers display in their efforts to depress demand for agricultural land. In general, a person's behavior is assumed to be rational when attempts are made to maximize wealth. When farmers seek to exclude NRAs from purchasing farmland, are they acting rationally? An extended analysis leads to the answer.

Farmers may be classified as owners of large farms, owners of small farms (defined as the size that is at or near the minimum acreage required in their locality to take advantage of all relevant economies of scale), or renters of large or small farms. Some overlapping will occur among these categories; for example, the owner of a small farm operation may also rent land from a neighbor. However, farmers whose farms would be in the small-farm-owner classification would often be referred to as family farmers. Some owners of small farms seek to gradually expand their acreage by purchasing or renting acreage near or adjoining their farms.[5] Of farmland transfers that take place each year, the majority occur among farmers. In 1976, for example, 65 percent of all farmland transferred went to active farmers, and farm enlargement accounted for 63 percent of all farm-tract purchases.[6]

This demand for additional farmland is motivated by an effort to increase the land base of the minimum-size farm so that all relevant economies of scale for acreage, machinery, and labor inputs may be realized and returns to investment maximized. Research shows that the minimum acreage requirement has increased over time, primarily because of changes in technology (see table 4-2).

But farmland also has value other than as a productive asset. In the decade of the 1970s, the value of farmland as an investment outstripped its value as a productive asset. Between 1972 and 1976, potential capital gains

Table 4–2
Numbers of Farms and Average Farm Size

Year	Number of Farms (thousands)	Average Acreage per Farm
1979	2,330	450
1975	2,491	427
1964	3,158	352

Source: *Statistical Abstract of the United States.* 100th Ed., 1979. Department of Commerce, Bureau of the Census (Washington, D.C.: U.S. Government Printing Office, 1979).

on all U.S. farmland totaled an estimated $339 billion; income earned from the products produced from that land totaled $144 billion, less than half the potential capital gain.[7]

To understand whether farmers who propose and lobby for restrictive legislation act rationally, there is a need to first understand how the trends just cited affect family farmers.

Farmers and Their Land: The Importance of Human Capital

Other things being equal, probably no other single resource is as immune from the vagaries of world events as land; land is a *store of value.*[8] This aspect of farmland influences the decisions of owners of farms. A farmer who desires to maximize net wealth would favor restraints on the overall demand for land under only one condition, if demand for land could be manipulated so that the farmer gained a strategic advantage in the role of land speculator. When a net-wealth-maximizing farmer is unable to manipulate the market, attempts to restrict the demand side of the market are fruitless.

When farmland is considered in the farmer's production process as a *factor of production*, conditions emerge to make farmer-supported restrictions on NRA ownership of farmland consistent with assumed rationality. Two conditions must be satisfied: farmers in total must be net demanders of farmland, and marginal benefits that accrue as a result of restrictions must outweigh marginal costs of achieving regulation.

That segment of the farm population comprised of active or potential sellers of land will prefer unrestricted demand in order to maximize the increase in land prices as a means of reaping capital gains on the value of their landholdings. For these farmers, the production factor aspect of their land does not function as a binding constraint on their behavior because they desire to sell their land.

When farmers as net demanders of farmland want to purchase additional acreage, whether for speculative or productive purposes, they have a
legitimate interest in attempting to manipulate the market so that they may
obtain such land at relatively favorable prices. Basically, the owners of
small farms demand land for two reasons: as a response to maximizing their
net wealth over the course of their occupation of farming, and in response
to the effects changes in technology impose on the earning power of their
farms. As a result, owners of small farms who want more agricultural land
for use as a factor of production in their business may not act to maximize,
at all times, the present value of their holdings (and clearly, farmers suffer
foregone capital gains as a result of restrictions against foreign participation
in the domestic farmland market). The reason is that costs are associated
with occupational mobility for all persons, and especially so for farmers,
whether the change is to another occupation within farming and agriculture, or to a completely different occupational group.

Among the farmers farming in 1962, roughly 82 percent had fathers
who were farmers.[9] This high degree of family occupational continuity is
explained by Laband and Lentz in terms of the comparative advantage farm
youths obtain in the occupation of farming as a by-product of growing up
on a farm, relative to otherwise identical, nonfarm youths.[10] Farmers impart to their children farm-specific knowledge about their particular farming operations. Much of this knowledge concerns qualities associated with
the land. Familiarity with the way productivity of the land is affected by
vagaries of weather, by fertilization, and by other inputs and processes is
knowledge specific to each tract of farmland. A youth assists his or her
father with the farming operations. Such youths acquire, without out-of-
pocket cost, through experience and from their parents, information about
the farm—information that would otherwise be very costly to obtain
(through trial and error). By the time a farm youth reaches the age of, say,
eighteen—the age when most other youngsters are just starting to acquire
job-specific skills (through employee training programs) or more general
skills (through college)—a farm youth has acquired a major portion of the
knowledge critical for the occupation of farming. Thus, youths who choose
subsequently to work the family farm have farm-specific skills. These skills
would decline in value if required acreage expansion and the high costs of
farmland combined to force them out of the family farm business and into
the nonfarm job market. Consequently, a rise in the price of agricultural
land may adversely affect the value of a farmer's occupational knowledge
and skill—the human capital factor.

Consider a typical farmer who owns a small farm, an acreage of land
that, in the community within which the farm lies, enables the farmer to
provide for his family. Such a farmer, if he desires to improve his standard
of living, is forced to either expand his operations by purchasing or renting

more land, or to sell his operation and become a tenant farmer or farm manager, or to completely change his occupation. In any capacity other than as a farm owner, the value of the farmer's farm-specific knowledge and skill is lower than when he is the owner of his own farm; because, at the same time a change occurs that forces him off his farm, he also forgoes any further potential capital gains on the value of farmland owned.

Why Restrictive Regulation?

Insofar as the vast majority of farmers resemble the small farmer portrayed above, and insofar as a large percentage of farmers opt to *attempt* to expand their holdings of farmland, restricting the demand for farmland would be in their economic interest—provided that the marginal gain, in relative terms of lower purchase prices for land, exceeds the marginal cost of obtaining regulation. In addition, as has been argued, net returns to a farmer as farm renter or as a farm manager are lower than the returns to the farmer as owner. If a beleaguered farmer sells out and leases the previously owned land back from a new owner, the landlord can then extract, in the form of higher rent, some percentage of the value of the specialized farm-specific occupational knowledge and skill that ties a farmer as tenant to the specific tract of land. Returns to farmers as tenants or managers are also lower than returns to them as owners because as tenants or managers they bear fewer risks than as owners. To the extent that shirking is reflected in salary, farmer-managers will earn even less. Finally, farmers as renters or managers reap none of the capital gains on the value of the land farmed.

The basic point is this: a rise in the price of land adversely affects the value of farmers' human capital. The reason is that increases in land prices reduce the ability of farmers who are seeking to operate farms with efficient minimum-size acreage to acquire any additional acreage needed to have an optimum investment pattern, the pattern needed to remain competitive. Because a farmer's human capital has significantly lower value in other occupational opportunities than in farming the family farm, exit from the occupation of farming is costly, and farmers resist such a change. In the extreme case, forced exit from the occupation of farming is accompanied by a complete loss in the value of the farmer's human capital; that is, his or her farm-specific knowledge and skills would be of no value in a totally different occupation. With respect, then, to farming as an occupation, maximization of net capital corresponds to maximization of long-run net wealth. This assumption regarding farmers' behavior provides a rationale for their push for restrictive legislation against NRAs and satisfies the precept of their rational behavior.

Only when the long-run, life cycle approach is considered does the consistency of the farmers' efforts to restrict any portion of the demand for land and their desire to maximize net wealth become evident. In the short run, such restrictions are costly, both in terms of forgone capital gains on the value of their own current landholdings and resources devoted to lobbying. At any given time, regulation of demand for farmland would appear (on paper) to indicate a strategy that does not maximize net wealth. Such appearances are deceptive. Restrictive legislation, such as that which imposes restraints on nonresident alien ownership of U.S. farmland, is compatible, in the long run, with the assumption of rational economic behavior on the part of U.S. farmers. Restrictions on the demand for land, or inducements to supply of land, result ultimately in a decrease in prices for land and reduce costs for acreage expansion, relative to the costs of such expansion in the absence of farmers' successful lobbying efforts. The rational farmer is presumed to pursue these lobbying efforts up to the point where the discounted, expected net marginal benefits just equal the marginal costs of doing so.

The point should not be misconstrued. The argument is not that owners of small farms simply demand farmland and do not ever supply farmland; many do, in fact, sell out. However, until the moment they decide to sell, restrictions on NRAs will be favored by owners of small farms as part of their net-capital-maximizing strategy with respect to their chosen occupation of farming.

From the preceding argument, we may also conclude, however, that a large NRA land-purchasing presence in the U.S. land market—one that contributes significantly to a tremendous rate of increase in land prices—will be largely ignored by farmers, and that they will make no effort to restrict purchases of farmland. Such conditions would cause gains on the physical capital assets (the land itself) to swamp the losses on farmers' human capital. At least some farmers would respond by selling out, going to the beach or the equivalent, and living off of their capital gains.

An example may be useful. Suppose that NRA participation in the market for U.S. agricultural land was, by itself, sufficient to create an increase in land prices of 100 percent per year, and that the general rate of inflation was running at a scant 5 percent per year. Gains on the value of farmers' landholdings would far outstrip losses to the value of farmers' human capital. In fact, farmers could afford (easily) to lose the entire value of their farm-specific human capital by quitting their farming and borrowing against their yearly capital gains, and live very comfortably at that. Sometimes this happens on the so-called urban fringe.

Small changes in land prices, however, are not sufficient to permit the change in value of capital gains to overwhelm the loss in value of the human capital. Below some threshold amount, small changes in land prices may thus do owners of small farms more harm than good; regulation then emerges as a vehicle to restore the rate of land-price increase to the perceived optimal trend in terms of maximizing the net wealth of owners of small farms. Thus, the answer to why there are restraints on NRA participation in the domestic farmland market is this: regulation of nonresident aliens occurs precisely *because* their incidence of participation in the market for U.S. farmland is small, not in spite of it.

For farmers to restrict other U.S. citizens or resident aliens from buying farmland would almost certainly be too costly politically, even though farmers might wish to do so in an effort to restrict demand and keep land prices low. The political cost of legislating against foreigners is undoubtedly considerably less.[11] Net benefits to family farmers in terms of lower land prices or reduced rates of farmland price inflation may outweigh the costs associated with lobbying for restrictive legislation, *on the margin*. This explains why nonresident aliens are targets of regulation, because the cost of discriminating against them is relatively low from the standpoint of both individual farmers and their lobbying organizations. This undoubtedly explains why restrictive legislation has been introduced in so many states, even though farmers are well represented only in certain state legislatures. Obtaining votes against NRAs either directly, or indirectly, by putting the real or imagined fear of such investors in the minds of the voting public, does not cost much to farmers, lobbyists, or politicians. Demand for regulation, like other normal goods, varies inversely with the cost of obtaining it.

Concluding Comments

Regulation, then, emerges out of a struggle between large farmers as net suppliers of farmland, and small, family farmers as net demanders of farmland, for the economic rents associated with marginal land-price changes resulting from participation of nonresident aliens in the market for U.S. farmland. With perhaps one exception, all of the states listed in table 4-1 are dominated by the agricultural sector, which is, in turn, dominated by farmers with small farm units. This provides us with the answer to why restrictions are targeted only at NRA ownership of farmland, but not other real estate or businesses. Restrictive regulations are targeted toward NRA ownership of U.S. farmland because it is in the economic interest of farmers who own small farms to eliminate that component of the demand for farmland. The incidence of state laws mandating restrictions on NRA purchase of farmland is indicative of the winning group in this game of rent-seeking. Apparently there is no group that finds it worth the political cost to restrict NRAs from the purchase of urban land in the United States.

Notes

1. *Monitoring Foreign Ownership of U.S. Real Estate,* Vol. 1 (USDA, Economics and Statistics Service, 1979), p. 1.

2. Ibid., p. 2.

3. Information on special-interest support for and opposition to laws restricting NRA participation in the domestic real estate market was obtained in response to a request for such information made in 1981 to each of the secretaries of state and attorneys general of the fifty states.

4. Seminal works on the subject of human capital in the economics literature are Gary S. Becker, "Investment in Human Capital: A Theoretical Analysis," *Journal of Political Economy* (October 1962); and Jacob Mincer, "Investment in Human Capital and Personal Income Distribution," *Journal of Political Economy* (August 1958).

5. Acreage that is spread in widely separated tracts becomes very costly to operate, since so much time gets taken up in movement from one plot to the next.

6. *Foreign Investment in the United States*, Practising Law Institute (Series No. 297, 1979), p. 352.

7. Ibid.

8. Many aspects of land are not discussed in this treatment of foreign ownership. For a more detailed treatment of land, see J.P. Marshall, "Land: Services and Property," No. 35 (November 1977) in *Land: Issues and Problems* Virginia Cooperative Extension Service, Virginia Tech.

9. P.M. Blau and O.D. Duncan, *The American Occupational Structure* (New York: John Wiley, 1967), p. 39.

10. D.N. Laband and B.F. Lentz, "Occupational Inheritance in Agriculture," *American Journal of Agricultural Economics* (May 1983).

11. Farm lobby organizations can gain valuable publicity by raising the specter of NRA control over U.S. agriculture. The paranoia associated with such an event makes much publicity. As a result, the cost of obtaining political support against NRAs becomes very inexpensive for lobbyists.

5

The Supply of Regulation

The Distributional Issue

As depicted in chapter 4, regulation of foreign ownership of U.S. farmland emerges out of a struggle between large farmers (as net suppliers of farmland) and small farmers (as net demanders of farmland) for the inframarginal rents associated with land-price changes that result from foreign participation in the market for U.S. farmland. Farmer-owners and farmer-renters push restrictive legislation as a rational response to incremental increases in the price of farmland that result from foreign bidding for agricultural land. Either of these groups would be considered to wield substantial political clout. Their gains, in the form of lower land prices, must come at the expense of farmers with large holdings of land who may be considered as net suppliers. It is evident that this group will be opposed to any attempts to restrict foreign (or domestic) purchases of farmland, and that the political power wielded by this group is also potentially great.

The nature of the gains or losses that accrue to small and large farmers as a result of regulation are depicted in figures 5–1 though 5–4.

Figure 5–1 depicts the market clearing price per acre and quantity of farmland demanded in competitive equilibrium, assuming the normal, downward-sloping demand-for-farmland curve, and an upward-sloping supply curve for farmland. Despite the fact that farmland is a quasi-static quantity, it is assumed that more suppliers are willing to sell as the price per acre rises, or, to say the same thing in a different way, the quantity supplied will be greater at higher prices than at lower prices.[1] At price per acre (p) the number of acres of land demanded exactly equals the number of acres that suppliers are willing to sell (q).

The first of two effects engendered by restricting foreign ownership of farmland is shown in figure 5–2. The restrictions act to remove a certain portion, albeit a small one, from the demand side of the market for agricultural real estate. The restricted demand for farmland curve, i.e., after institution of legal restrictions, (D'), lies everywhere below the previous demand curve, (D). The new equilibrium quantity of land transferred is q' at a price p'. Relative to the situation where foreigners were allowed into the domestic land market, demanders of land are better off. Their gain in consumers' surplus is equal to the trapezoidal area $pp'ab$.

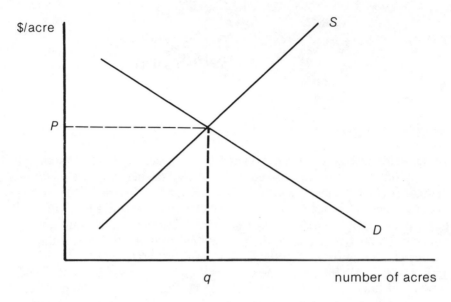

Figure 5-1. Market Clearing Price per Acre and Quantity of Farmland

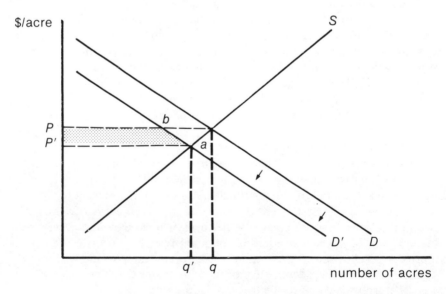

Figure 5-2. The Impact of State Restrictions on the Demand for Farmland

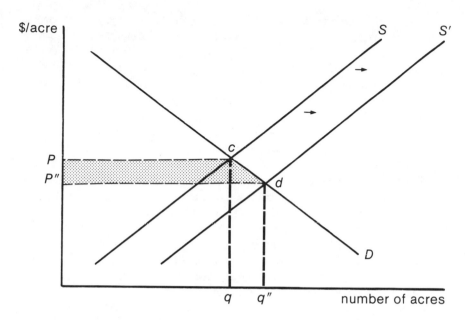

Figure 5-3. The Impact of State Restrictions on the Supply of Farmland

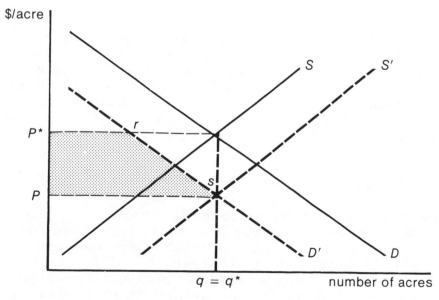

Figure 5-4. The Net Impact of State Restrictions in Terms of Prices Paid
by Domestic Farmers

The second effect of restrictive legislation derives from one specific form of the regulation—complete prohibition of landownership by a non-resident alien. Such a law would force foreigners to either become U.S. citizens or else sell off their U.S. landholdings. To the extent this latter option is chosen, there will be an increase in the supply of land in the short run, which is exhibited in figure 5-3. The supply curve shifts outward from S to S' with the influx of new sellers, and the new equilibrium price and quantity of land sold are p'' and q'', respectively. Domestic farmers as demanders of farmland are the recipients of consumers' surplus in the amount of $pp''cd$.

The combined supply and demand effects are illustrated in figure 5-4. The deletion from the demand side of the market is noted, as is the addition to the supply side of the market. For graphical simplicity the curves are drawn in such a way that the equilibrium quantity of land that changes hands remains constant (q). Note that before regulation some portion of q was purchased by foreigners; after regulation all of q is bought domestically because domestic farmers are encouraged to buy more land as a result of the drop in price from p to p^*. There has been a net transfer of wealth from sellers of land to buyers of land, which is equivalent to the trapezoid pp^*rs. Sellers lose the value of the capital gains they would have reaped by selling at higher prices, while demanders of farmland are able to buy at lower prices.

This model suggests that the pattern of legislation that restricts foreign ownership of U.S. farmland can be explained in terms of the relative political power of these two interest groups of farmers, as they fight over the inframarginal rents associated with the sale of farmland. It also suggests an answer to one of the questions posed in chapter 4, namely, why restrictions are targeted specifically at domestic farmland rather than at all real estate investment undertaken by foreigners. In this model, the principal protagonists are concerned only with sales of farmland, to the exclusion of other types of foreign investment. It is strictly a distributional struggle among farmers, and a couple of other groups as interested parties.

Casual Support for the Model

This public-choice model, in which the incidence of restrictive legislation is partially determined by the relative political power held by two opposing groups of farmers, tends to be supported widely by observable events in the state legislatures. The letters I received from the offices of the secretaries of state and attorneys general for the fifty states invariably included some comment to the effect that some farm organization or another was behind the push for restrictive legislation. Introductory comments to a number of bills introduced in the state legislatures cite the danger to the family farm as a motivation for passage. One particular reply, from Jack Gibbons of the Delaware Legislative Council, proved illuminating. Gibbons details the case of a farmer/legislator who sponsored legislation in the state House of Representatives to restrict farmland ownership by nonresident aliens. Though passed by the House, the bill was killed by the Senate in response to pressure from large, local farmers who were apparently negotiating sales with foreign purchasers at very favorable prices.

One additional interest group is mentioned consistently as being against restriction of foreign ownership of land—the Association of Realtors. Their motivation is obvious: Realtors make their living from turnover of real estate. Protective legislation hits them where it hurts the most, in the pocketbook. Small, family farmers, under technologically induced pressure to expand their acreage holdings, will seek to inhibit the demand for land in their respective states whenever the expected marginal benefits, in terms of securing an optimal rate of land-price increase, exceed the costs of successfully lobbying their state legislature for protection from outsiders. If it can be assumed that restricting foreign ownership of farmland yields benefits, in the form of lower land prices, that exceed the cost of lobbying, then one implication of the model is that the pattern of restrictive state legislation can be explained in terms of the relative political power of small farmers on the one hand, and large farmers and Realtors on the other. That is, effective supply of regulation is a function of the lobbying strength of two competing interest groups. This implication is tested in the following section.

The Politics of Redistribution: Testing the Model

Because a distinct pattern of legislation which restricts NRAs from ownership of farmland has already emerged in several states, it seems reasonably certain that some subset of the population will gain from it—one that certainly includes small, family farmers who are net demanders of farmland. A number of additional states have instituted reporting requirements with respect to NRA ownership or purchase of farmland. The effect of such laws is probably minimal, especially with respect to aliens whose home countries are not concerned about the flight of capital out of the country. However, a certain percentage of potential farm buyers may be discouraged from buying since anonymity is sometimes quite valuable. The unauthorized removal of capital from Italy is illegal, as it is in a number of other countries. Penalties for engaging in such transfers can include heavy fines and/or jail sentences. It therefore behooves potential investors from overseas to restrict their investments to projects that can ensure, via institutional structure, their anonymity. Up until 1978, when the AFIDA was enacted by the U.S. Congress, domestic farmland was considered to be one such safe investment. The passage of the AFIDA and numerous laws at the state level that mandate reporting requirements for ownership, purchase, or sale of land by foreigners, may mitigate substantially the value that foreigners place on U.S. land.

In addition, potential farm buyers may be driven away from an investment in U.S. farmland because the costs associated with compliance with the reporting requirements may be enough to turn a marginal investment into a submarginal one.

Two classes of factors are involved in attempting to predict whether or not the small farmers in any specific state will be successful in their quest to restrict foreign ownership of farmland: the political clout enjoyed by small farmers *relative* to that enjoyed by large farmers and Realtors; and the *absolute* amount of political power obtainable by small farmers, a factor governed by institutional and demographic factors.

This latter class is explored by McCormick and Tollison.[2] They argue that the success of influence-buying in state legislatures is affected by a number of factors, including the size of the legislature, the ratio of the sizes of the two chambers in bicameral legislatures, and the size and per-capita income of the state's population. Agricultural interests must be well represented in the state legislature, because either the number of farmers relative to the entire state population is large—the vote-counting theory of influence—or else because agriculture represents a substantial portion of the state's income—the vote-buying theory of influence, as amended by McCormick and Tollison. Applying this criterion to the pattern of state restrictions against NRAs, there is a high degree of consistency between the presence of regulation and the strength of agricultural interests in the state. In particular, there should be no restrictions, or perhaps minor ones (reporting requirements), in states where agriculture is a minor occupation, measured by numbers of farmers or by farm income as a percentage of total state income. This finding squares nicely with their model. It should not necessarily be the case however, that a preponderance of agriculture in a state, however measured, will ensure restrictions on foreign ownership of land, since those agricultural interests must then overcome opposition in the legislature.

All other things being equal, there should be an inverse relationship between the success of small farmers in obtaining regulation and the political clout wielded by opposition groups. That is, relative power factors will also affect political outcomes. The opposition is headed by individual farmers with large holdings of land, the National Association of Realtors, and, occasionally, by a state chamber of commerce. States in which the Association of Realtors is large are, in fact, virtually free of any type of farmland regulation.

In the case of California, for example, the agricultural interest is extremely powerful and foreigners are purchasing a great deal of farmland in the state, yet no restrictions have been imposed so far. The explanation for this lack of regulation is CAR, the California Association of Realtors. This organization is particularly powerful in that state, as might be predicted, and has managed to successfully oppose the several attempts that have been made to prohibit foreign ownership of farmland. This pattern of successful opposition extends throughout the so-called sun belt, where recent population inmigration has incited a boom in the real estate industry, and a consequent strengthening of the political power enjoyed by the states' real estate associations.

The shift in political power in favor of real estate organizations in the sun belt states is illustrated by the state of Arizona. In 1978 the Arizona legislature repealed existing restrictions against foreign purchase of real estate. Since that time several new bills that seek to reimpose those restrictions have been introduced into the legislature, but none has been heard successfully.

However, farmers have been powerful enough in certain states to lobby successfully for additional protective legislation. It was argued in chapter 4 that the family farmers' push for protective legislation occurs because expected net benefits outweigh current lobbying costs, on the margin. They would undoubtedly prefer to curtail the *domestic* component of demand as well, but this can only be accomplished at a high cost. Several of the states have legislated restrictions on corporate ownership of farmland as well as foreign ownership. If the model presented in chapter 4 is an accurate depiction of reality, these restrictions could only be enacted in states where the small-farmer segment of the population is not only politically powerful in relation to large farmers and real estate agents, but with respect to the non-farming population as well.

Observable events confirm the rent-seeking theory of corporate land-ownership restrictions. The states with such restrictions currently on the books are Iowa, Kansas, Minnesota, Missouri, Nebraska, North Dakota, Oklahoma, South Dakota, and Wisconsin. These are all states in which the primary occupation is agriculture. There is no significant nonagricultural industry to oppose imposition of corporate prohibitions on landownership. Family farmers represent a substantial proportion of the population in each of these states, ensuring that agricultural interests receive due attention in the legislative body. It should come as no surprise then to learn that the main proponents of regulation of corporate ownership of farmland were the state affiliations of the national farmer's organizations.

It has been argued that the rent-seeking model of farmland regulation implies that the observed pattern of legal restrictions can be explained by the relative political strength of the two opposing factions relative to each other, and by the relative importance of agriculture to the state in question. This dependency is modeled formally in equation 5.1 and explained below.

$$REG = a_0 + a_1FL + a_2RGNP + a_3YPC + a_4POP + a_5RFR + \mu, \quad (5.1)$$

where REG = 0–1 variable that indicates the presence (1) or absence (0) of a major restriction against NRA ownership of farmland;

FL = the proportion of the state legislature that is composed of farmers;

$RGNP$ = the proportion of total state income that is derived from farming;

YPC = per-capita state income;

POP = state population;

RFR = the number of farmers in the state divided by the number of Realtors in the state; and

μ = a random disturbance term.

Major restrictions against NRA ownership of farmland typically take one of two forms: direct restrictions regarding the quantity of acreage that a nonresident alien may legally obtain title to, and time limits on holdings. The effect of the latter regulation is to drive up the cost to aliens of holding land, thus reducing the profitability of investment, shifting the total demand for farmland down. South Carolina has an official acreage restriction of 500,000 acres, which is treated as a nonrestriction since it is nonbinding—no foreigner comes close to owning even one-tenth of that amount.

As discussed previously, there are two sets of factors that help determine the degree and success of rent-seeking efforts in the state legislatures: institutional/demographic factors and relative power factors. The institutional/demographic variables are concerned with the cost to any specific interest group of buying influence.

One measure of the costs associated with achieving regulation is the percentage of the seats in the legislature that are held by farmers. The presumption is that a farmer/legislator can marshall support for (or opposition to) a farmland-regulation bill at a much lower cost than can an ordinary farmer. For one thing, he or she obtains one legislative vote for free—his or her own. Second, a farmer/legislator can engage in logrolling with other politicians as a means of obtaining additional legislative votes; a method unavailable to farmers or real estate agents who are not also legislators. Before this variable can be given a positive or negative sign there must be some presumption as to whether small farmers or large farmers are most likely to be legislators. However, no such distinction is readily apparent. On the one hand, small farmers receive considerable support from the state affiliates of the national farm organizations, which enhances their electability to public office. On the other hand, this distribution of power works to the disadvantage of larger farmers whenever their views differ from those of small farmers. Becoming a legislator may be the least-cost method for large farmers to obtain legislative influence in the face of organizational opposition. In addition, large farmers are better able to combine the occupation of farming with legislating than can small farmers. The presumption here is that a large farmer employs a manager or other trustworthy employee to run the farm, while the small farmer is highly dependent on his or her own labor. Unless the legislative sessions meet during the off-season, the opportunity cost of serving in the legislature will therefore be higher for the small farmer than for the large one. If legislatures are dominated by small farmers/legistlators, *FL* should sign positive, and vice versa if large farmers make up the bulk of farmer/legislators. Because it is unclear a priori which of these effects dominates, the variable will remain unsigned for the present.

A second measure of the relative importance of agriculture to the referent state, an indirect predictor of farmers' influence in the state capital, is the percentage of state income that is generated in the farming sector (*RGNP*). Because for most crops the large majority of total output is produced on small, family farms, it is predicted that this variable will be positively related to the incidence of restrictive legislation.

As argued by McCormick and Tollison (1980), the wealth of a state's population (as proxied by income per capita *YPC*) influences lobbying in two ways. The costs to individual voters of monitoring the political process increase as wealth increases (a substitution effect). The ability of a lobby group to use the political process to redistribute income in its favor should thus rise in wealthier jurisdictions. However, an income effect cuts in the opposite direction. Monitoring the political process may also be an income-elastic good, which is indulged in more frequently in wealthier districts, decreasing the effectiveness of special interest groups.

McCormick and Tollison predict the substitution effect to dominate and their wealth variable has the correct sign, even if it is insignificant. This provides some reason to expect *YPC* to be related positively to *REG*.

McCormick and Tollison also argue that more wealth transfers of the type discussed in this chapter will be forthcoming in large populations than in small ones. As population in the specific political jurisdiction grows, the probability that any one voter can influence collective decisions decreases. Moreover, the per-capita cost-share of any given transfer that is borne by an individual declines as population increases. For both reasons we expect *POP* to have a positive sign.

It is difficult to separate the net demanders of farmland from the net suppliers of farmland, given available agricultural statistics. Therefore, no reliable measure of the relative political power of large farmers as opposed to small farmers is presented. However, it is possible to measure the relative political clout of farmers as a whole (assumed to be dominated by the 95 percent who are small farmers) versus real estate interests, which provides the bulk of the organized resistance to regulation of the agricultural real estate market.

One measure of the comparative political clout wielded by each of these groups is provided by a simple head count, by state, of the numbers of Realtors and farmers (proxied by the number of farms). It is predicted that the ratio of farmers to Realtors will be related positively to the presence of legal restriction of foreign ownership of domestic farmland. That is, the more that farmers outnumber, and hence can out-vote Realtors, the greater the likelihood that the farmers' quest for protective legislation will not be thwarted by Realtors.

Two versions of the model presented in equation (5.1) were estimated using the logit procedure for ordinary least squares, where the dependent variable is dichotomous. Classical least-squares estimation provides inefficient estimates of the coefficients because of heteroscedasticity in the variances. The logit procedure provides efficient estimators, and the estimated value of the endogenous variable REG is the conditional probability of regulation, given the values of the dependent variables. The results of the estimation procedure are reported in table 5-1.

The estimates strongly support the contention that the presence of restrictive legislation against NRA ownership of U.S. farmland is related positively to the political power wielded by farmers, relative to Realtors and relative to the public at large, as measured by RFR and FL, respectively. In both specifications of the model the coefficients on these two variables are positive, as expected, and significant. It should be noted that the positive sign on FL can be taken as evidence that farmer/legislators are predominately small farmers. The importance of agriculture to total state income is related positively to incidence of restrictive legislation, as expected, but the coefficient is insignificant. Finally, the estimates of POP and YPC provide unmistakable support for the McCormick–Tollison analysis that suggests that population is partially responsible for the level of economic regulation, and that the substitution effect dominates the income effect with respect to the manner in which per-capita income affects regulatory activity. In both cases the variable coefficients were significantly positive as predicted.

Concluding Comments

The rent-seeking model presented in chapter 4 has been shown in this chapter to provide a reasonably powerful explanation for the observed pattern of state restriction of NRA ownership of U.S. agricultural land.

Small landholders or renters who are net demanders of farmland, for technological reasons rationally seek to purchase additional farmland at the

Table 5-1
Logit Regression Results for Major Restriction (1976)

Explanatory Variable	Coefficient/Chi-Square	
Constant	-16.978795[a]	- 15.588080[a]
	(5.26)	(5.44)
RFR[c]	0.276664	0.291910[a]
	(4.01)	(4.51)
YPC[d]	0.001469[b]	0.001377[b]
	(3.09)	(3.17)
FL[e]	0.385407[a]	0.397652[a]
	(4.26)	(4.84)
POP[f]	0.000040[a]	0.000035[a]
	(4.26)	(3.91)
RGNP[g]	10.253244	
	(1.49)	
Redictive accuracy coefficient	0.604	0.588
Correct	88.0%	86.0%

[a]Significant at 0.05 level.

[b]Significant at 0.10 level.

[c]*USDA 1974 Census of Agriculture,* vol. 1, Pts. 1–50 (1977) and National Association of Realtors, *Membership Report* (1975) (Washington, D.C.: U.S. Government Printing Office).

[d]U.S. Department of Commerce, Bureau of the Census; *Statistical Abstract of the U.S.* (Washington, D.C.: U.S. Government Printing Office, 1976).

[e]Insurance Information Institute, *Occupational Profile of State Legislators* (New York; 1976).

[f]*Statistical Abstract* (1976) U.S. Department of Commerce, Bureau of the Census; *Statistical Abstract of the U.S.* (Washington, D.C.: U.S. Government Printing Office, 1976).

[g]*USDA 1974 Census of Agriculture,* vo. 1, Pts. 1–50 (1977) and U.S. Department of Commerce, Bureau of the Census; *Statistical Abstract of the U.S.* (Washington, D.C.: U.S. Government Printing Office, 1976).

cheapest per-acre price possible. Accordingly, they lobby for protective legislation (acreage or other restrictions) as long as perceived returns in the form of lower land prices exceed the cost of lobbying. Owners of small, family farms realize that lower land prices are obtainable by restricting access of foreigners to the doemstic land market, which shifts both the demand and supply curves for farmland in directions considered favorable. Large farmers and real estate agents oppose these restrictions because, for large farmers, restrictions mitigate against high capital gains to investment in land, and for real estate agents, restrictions inhibit their means of livelihood. The incidence of restrictive regulation is indicative of the winning group in this struggle for redistribution of income. It appears in this case that numbers weigh more heavily than dollars in the acquisition of political power, at least in the state legislatures.

The findings of the last two chapters are considerably at odds with those of several USDA studies conducted in the mid to late 1970s. These studies (correctly) found an incidence of foreign ownership of farmland in the

the United States that was exceedingly small, but incorrectly concluded that the impact of foreign ownership of U.S. farmland was too minute to warrant regulation. It appears, however, that family farmers find regulation of U.S. farmland ownership to be in their economic best interest, and that regulation at the state level is the most cost-effective way to restrict the foreign presence in the market for U.S. agricultural land.

Notes

1. One can add to the quantity of farmland through such activities as draining marshes and adding fill dirt.

2. Robert E. McCormick and Robert D. Tollison, "Wealth Transfers in a Representative Democracy," in *Toward a Theory of the Rent Seeking Society,* J.M. Buchanan, R.D. Tollison, and G. Tullock, eds. (College Station: Texas A&M University Press, 1980).

6

A Survey of State Restrictions and Reporting Requirements

This chapter consists of two sections. The first section, a state-by-state survey, is a compilation of existing state legislation, current to October 1983, relating to the legal status of foreign and corporate investment in U.S. real estate.[1] The second section examines the efforts of the various states to enforce these statutes.

State Summaries

The restrictive statutes cited in the state-by-state survey are divided into three main classes: (1) Aliens—General restrictions; (2) Aliens—Reporting requirements; and (3) Corporate restrictions. The general restrictions pertain to statutes designed to directly limit foreign ownership of U.S. agricultural real estate. The reporting requirements include provisions that require nonresident aliens (or corporations with a certain percentage of shareholders who are aliens) with an interest in U.S. real estate to report information about that interest to some state governmental authority. Corporate restrictions concern restraints imposed on both foreign and domestic corporations with respect to ownership rights they may legally possess in certain types of real property.

There are thirty states with some type of law restricting nonresident alien ownership of U.S. farmland. Eight states have instituted reporting requirements for aliens with landholdings therein. Thirteen states have restrictions on corporate farming and/or bar business entities from owning agricultural land.

Restrictions against foreigners encompass both foreign individuals and foreign corporations. Corporate restrictions are targeted at domestic corporations in excess of (usually) ten members.

Alabama

Aliens—General restrictions. None.

Aliens—Reporting requirements. None.

Corporate restrictions. Foreign corporations must file a certified copy of their articles of incorporation prior to transacting business in the State. Ala. Code § 10-2-250 (1977).

Alaska

Aliens—General restrictions. Mining rights may be acquired only by adult citizens, aliens who have declared their intention to become citizens, aliens whose home countries grant reciprocal treatment, and certain corporations. Alaska Stat. §§ 38.190 (1973).

Aliens—Reporting requirements. None.

Corporate restrictions. Articles of incorporation must include the name and address of each affiliate that is a nonresident alien or a corporation whose place of incorporation is outside the United States. Alaska Stat. § 10.05.255 (1979) supp.). A certificate of authority must be obtained by a foreign corporation prior to transacting business in the state. The application must include (1) the name and address of each affiliate that is a nonresident alien or corporation whose place of incorporation is outside the United States, and the percentage of outstanding shares controlled by each affiliate; and (2) the name and address of a person owning at least 5 percent of any class of shares owned by that person. Alaska Stat. §§ 10.050615, 10.05.702 (1979 supp.).

Arizona

Aliens—General restrictions. None.

Aliens—Reporting requirements. None.

Corporate restrictions. Foreign corporations must obtain a certificate of authority prior to transacting business in the state (model code disclosures). Ariz. Rev. Stat. Ann. §§ 10-110, 10-106 (1975). All corporations must file annual reports (model code disclosures and names of shareholders holding more than 20 percent of any class of shares, including persons beneficially holding shares through nominees). Ibid., § 10-125 (1975). No sales, leases, or subleases of state land shall be made to corporations or associations not qualified to transact business in this state. Ibid., § 37-240B (supp. 1980-81). No individual, corporation, or association may purchase more than 160 acres of agricultural land or more than 640 acres of grazing land. Ariz. Const. art. 10, §§ 11, Ariz. Rev. Stat. § 37-240(A) (supp. 1980–81).

Arkansas

Aliens—General restrictions. Resident aliens may acquire any interest in real estate. Nonresident aliens may acquire any interest in any real estate except agricultural land. The restrictions set forth in this act do not apply to agricultural land acquired by a foreign party for immediate or potential use for nonfarming purposes. 1979 Ark. Acts, Art.1096, §§ 7,9,10. Aliens are ineligible to obtain a deed to tax forfeited agricultural land from the state until they are naturalized. Ark. Stat. Ann. § 10-926 (1976).

Aliens—Reporting requirements. Any foreign party or agent, trustee, or fiduciary for a foreign party who acquires any interest (except leases and options of less than ten years) in agricultural land in any manner, shall register such ownership in the office of the circuit clerk in the county in which the land is located, within sixty days after such acquisition. The registration shall include a description of the land acquired, and the name and business address of the foreign party that acquired such lands or on whose behalf the lands were acquired. The clerk shall record the information and forward copies of the registrations to the secretary of state. Ark. Stat. Ann. §§ 77-2203, 77-2204, 77-2211 (supp. 1979). There are a couple of exceptions to this statute. The attorney general may enforce the act by filing an action in the circuit court of the appropriate county. If the attorney general refuses to bring an action, any person claiming a violation may bring an action. If the court finds a violation of the act, it may order that the agricultural land be divested within two years to a nonforeign party. Any land not divested within two years shall be ordered sold at a public sale. Ibid., §§ 77-2205, 77-2206.

Corporate restrictions. Foreign corporations must file a copy of their articles of incorporation prior to transacting business in the state. Foreign corporations and other business entities are explicitly affected by the alien restrictions and reporting requirements listed for this state. Ark. Stat. Ann. § 64-1201 (supp. 1966 and 1977) and see earlier reference.

California

Aliens—General restrictions. Only persons who are citizens of the United States, or who have declared their intention of becoming citizens, or whose country grants reciprocal rights, or who are granted the right by treaty may be issued prospecting permits or leases on public lands. Alien corporations are not eligible for the above rights unless 90 percent or more of the shares are owned by eligible persons or corporations. Cal. Pub. Res. Code § 6801 (West 1977).

Only U.S. citizens or persons who have declared their intention to become such, and are also state residents, may purchase state-owned agricultural inland, lake, swamp, or overflowed lands. Cal. Pub. Res. Code § 7601 (West 1977).

Aliens—Reporting requirements. None.

Corporate restrictions. Foreign corporations must obtain a certificate of qualification prior to transacting business in the state (minimal disclosures).

All corporations must file annual reports (minimal disclosures). Cal. Corp. Code § 2108 (West 1977).

Colorado

Aliens—General restrictions. None.

Aliens—Reporting requirements. None.

Corporate restrictions. Foreign corporations must obtain a certificate of authority prior to transacting business in the state (model code disclosures). Colo. Rev. Stat. § 7-9-101 (1973). All corporations must file annual reports (model code disclosures). Ibid., § 7-10-101 (1973).

Connecticut

Aliens—General restrictions. Nonresident aliens are only authorized to hold and transmit real estate if it is used in mining and developing the products of the mine. Resident aliens and citizens of France may hold real estate without limitation but the right to citizens of France exists only so long as France accords the same rights to U.S. citizens. Conn. Gen. Stat. Ann. §§ 47-57, 47-58 (1978).

Aliens—Reporting requirements. None.

Corporate restrictions. Foreign corporations must obtain a certificate of authority prior to transacting business in the state (model code disclosures). Ibid., §§ 33-396, 33-399 (supp. 1978). Foreign corporations must file annual reports (model code disclosures). Ibid., § 33-406 (supp. 1978). Upon qualification, foreign corporations enjoy the same rights and privileges as domestic corporations. Additionally, a foreign corporation is authorized to purchase, hold, mortgage, lease, sell, and convey real estate "for its lawful uses and purposes" without having to qualify to transact business. Conn. Stat. Ann. § 33-401 (1958) and § 33-397 (supp. 1977).

Delaware

Aliens—General restrictions. Aliens are authorized to take, acquire, hold, and dispose of real property in the same manner as a citizen of the State. Del. Code Ann. tit. 25, § 306 (1974).

Aliens—Reporting requirements. None.

Corporate restrictions. Foreign corporations must register before doing business in the state. Foreign corporations must file annual reports (model code disclosures and amount of capital invested in real estate and other property). Del. Code Ann. tit. 8, §§ 371, 374 (1974).

District of Columbia

Aliens—General restrictions. None.

Aliens—Reporting requirements. None.

Corporate restrictions. Foreign corporations must obtain a certificate of authority before transacting business in the state (model code disclosures). D.C. Code Ann. § 29-933 (1973). Foreign corporations must file annual reports (model code disclosures). Ibid., § 29-933m (1973).

Florida

Aliens—General restrictions. Effective September 1, 1981, each alien corporation desiring to acquire any real property in the state shall have, prior to acquisition, and thereafter, a registered office and agent within the state. In addition, each alien corporation must file a report with the department of state between January 1 and July 1 of each year, giving identifying information. Any alien corporation that fails to meet these requirements shall not be entitled to own, purchase, or sell any real property in the state until there has been compliance with such requirements. 1981 Fla. Laws, § 943.468.

Aliens—Reporting requirements. See Aliens—General restrictions.

Corporate restrictions. Foreign corporations must register before doing business in the state. Foreign corporations must file annual reports (model code disclosures and amount of capital invested in real estate and other property). Fla. Stat. Ann. § 607.304 (1977). See also Aliens—General restrictions.

Georgia

Aliens—General restrictions. Aliens who are the subjects of governments at peace with the United States shall have the privilege of purchasing, holding, and conveying real estate. Ga. Code Ann. § 1-2-11 (1982).

Aliens—Reporting requirements. Same as Florida, see Ga. Code Ann. § 16-14-15 (1982).

Corporate restrictions. Foreign corporations must file a certificate of authority in order to transact business in the state (model code disclosures). Ga. Stat. Ann. § 22-1401 (1977).

Hawaii

Aliens—General restrictions. Persons seeking to lease or purchase either a residence lot on the island of Oahu from a development board or a residential house lot within a development tract within the control of the Hawaii development authority must have declared their intent to become citizens and are residents of Hawaii. Hawaii Rev. Stat. § 206.9 (1976).

A person applying to acquire state-owned farmland must have been a resident of the state at any time for at least three years. Hawaii Rev. Stat. § 171-68 (1976).

Aliens—Reporting requirements. None.

Corporate restrictions. Foreign corporations, prior to conducting business in the state, must file with the Director of the Regulatory Agencies a sworn disclosure statement (model code disclosures) and a copy of their articles of incorporation. Ibid., §§ 416-95, 418-9 (1976).

Idaho

Aliens—General restrictions. Only U.S. citizens and aliens who have declared their intention to become U.S. citizens may purchase state lands. Idaho Code § 58-313 (1976).

Aliens—Reporting requirements. None.

Corporate restrictions. Foreign corporations must file evidence of incorporation prior to transacting business in the state. All corporations organized or doing business in the state must file annual reports (model code disclosures). Ibid., §§ 30-601, 30-501 (supp. 1978).

Illinois

Aliens—General restrictions. "All aliens" are authorized to acquire, hold, inherit, alienate, sell, assign, encumber, devise, and convey lands, but they must dispose of such lands within six years (or, if under the age of twenty-one, within six years of reaching twenty-one), unless during the interim the alien obtains United States citizenship. The penalty is sale by the state with proceeds going to the state. Ill. Ann. Stat. ch. 6, §§ 1,2 (Smith-Hurd 1975, and supp. 1983–84). Alien landlords are prohibited from including payment of taxes as part of the direct or indirect rent due on a lease of farmlands. Ibid., § 9.

Aliens—Reporting requirements. Any foreign person who acquires or transfers any interest, other than a leasehold interest of five years or less, or a security interest, in agricultural land in this state shall submit a report to the Director of Agriculture not later than ninety days after the date of such acquisitions or transfer. Such report shall be submitted in such form and in accordance with such procedures as the director may require and shall contain:

1. the legal name and the address of such foreign person;
2. the citizenship of such foreign person;

3. the nature of the legal entity holding the interest, the country in which such foreign person is created or organized, and the principal place of business of such foreign person;
4. the type of interest in the agricultural land acquired or transferred;
5. the legal description and acreage of such agricultural land;
6. the purchase price paid for, or any other consideration given for, such interest;
7. the legal name and address of the person to whom such interest is transferred;
8. the agricultural purposes for which the foreign person intends to use the land; and
9. such other information as the director may require by regulation.

Ill. Stat. Ann. ch. 5, § 603(a) (Smith-Hurd supp. 1980)

Foreign persons holding agricultural land before the effective day of the act (September 14, 1979) should have reported such holdings within 180 days of such date, including in the report similar information to that listed above. Ibid., § 603(b).

When a person changes status to become a foreign person or when land changes to become agricultural land, reports must be filed within ninety days of the change in status as above. Ibid., § 603(d).

Foreign persons other than individuals and governments may be required to submit an additional report containing the names and addresses of persons holding an interest in such foreign person, and their citizenship, or the country where organized and the principal place of business. Entities whose names are disclosed in the additional report may have to further report the names of persons holding an interest in those entities. Ibid., § 603(f). Failure to report may result in a civil penalty imposed by the director, but such penalty, when added to the federal penalty for violation of the Agricultural Foreign Investment Disclosure Act of 1978 shall not exceed 25 percent of the fair market value of the interest in the land. Ibid., § 604.

The definitions are:

1. *agricultural land:* land used for agriculture, forestry, or timber production, except agricultural land used primarily to meet pollution control laws, and
2. *foreign person:* nonresident aliens, foreign governments, alien corporations, partnerships, trusts and other entities, and any corporation, partnership, trust, or other entity in which a significant interest is held by any combination of the foregoing. Ibid., § 602.

Corporate restrictions. Foreign corporations need a certificate of authority to transact business in the state (model code disclosures). Ill. Ann. Stat. ch.

32, § 157.102 (Smith-Hurd 1954). All corporations must file annual reports (model code disclosures) Ibid., § 157-115 (1954 and supp. 1978). Some corporations and other business entities are explicitly affected by the alien reporting requirements listed for this state.

Indiana

Aliens—General restrictions. Natural persons who are aliens, whether resident or nonresident, may acquire by purchase, devise, or descent any real estate, but any alien who shall acquire in excess of 320 acres must dispose of the excess within 5 years, unless he or she becomes a U.S. citizen, or the excess will escheat to the state. Ind. Code Ann. §§ 32-1-8-1, 32-1-8-2 (Burns 1973).

However, other sections provide that aliens who have not declared an intention to become U.S. citizens or who reside outside of Indiana may take and hold real estate only by devise and descent, and any alien may acquire land through enforcement of a debt or lien. All such lands must be divested within five years. Ibid., §§ 32-1-7-1, 32-1-7-2, 32-1-7-3.

Aliens—Reporting requirements. None.

Corporate restrictions. Foreign corporations must obtain a certificate of authority before transacting business in the state (model code disclosures). Ibid., § 23-1-11-1 (1972). All corporations must file annual reports (model code disclosures). Ibid., § 23-1-11-7 (1972).

Iowa

Aliens—General restrictions.

1. A nonresident alien, foreign business, or foreign government; or an agent, trustee, or fiduciary thereof shall not purchase or otherwise acquire any interest in agricultural land in the state. Iowa Code Ann. §§ 567.2, 567.3(1) (West 1983).
2. A person or business that acquires agricultural land, except by devise or descent, whose status changes to nonresident alien or foreign business, must divest itself of all interest in the land within two years of the change of status. Ibid., § 567.6.
3. Exceptions
   a. All those holding agricultural land on January 1, 1980, who would otherwise be restricted by this act, may continue to own or hold the land, but may not purchase or otherwise acquire additional agricultural land. Ibid., § 567.3(1).
   b. The restrictions do not apply to agricultural land acquired by devise or descent, but such land must be divested within two years of the acquisition. Ibid., §§ 567.3(3), 567.5.

    c.   The restrictions shall not apply to an interest in agricultural land, not to exceed 320 acres, acquired for an immediate or pending use other than farming. The land must be put into that use within five years after acquisition, and shall not be used for farming before being put to a nonfarming use, except under lease to one who is not subject to restrictions on agricultural landholdings. Ibid., §§ 567.3(3) and 567.4.

4.   Enforcement. The attorney general may bring an action in the district court of the country in which the land is located for land acquired in violation of the act. The court may declare the land be escheated to the state. Ibid., §§ 567.9, 567.10.5. Definitions

    a.   Agricultural land: land suitable for use in the production of agricultural crops, poultry, eggs, milk, fruit or other horticultural products, livestock, grazing, timber, forest products, nursery products, and sod. It does not include a contract where a processor of farm products provides farm services.

    b.   Foreign business: a corporation incorporated under the laws of a foreign country, or a business entity in which a majority interest is owned directly or indirectly by nonresident aliens. Legal entities including trusts do not affect the determination of ownership of a foreign business. Ibid., § 567.1.

Aliens—Reporting requirements. Nonresident aliens, corporations created under the laws of a foreign country, business entities in which a majority interest is owned directly or indirectly by nonresident aliens, or a foreign government that owns or acquires an interest in agricultural land must register the land with the secretary of state within sixty days. The registration shall contain the name of the owner and the location and number of acres. If the owner of the land is an agent, trustee, or fiduciary of a nonresident alien, foreign business, or foreign government, the registration shall contain the name of any principal for whom the land was purchased. Ibid., § 567.7.

A nonresident alien, foreign business, or foreign government acquiring agricultural land not subject to the restrictions of this act because the land was acquired for an immediate or pending use other than farming shall file a report with the secretary of state before March 31 of each year. The report shall contain the following: (1) the name of the owner of the land or owner of the interest in the land; (2) if the land is owned by an agent, trustee, or fiduciary of a nonresident alien, foreign business, or foreign government, the name of any principal for whom the land was purchased; (3) the location and number of acres; (4) the date the land or the interest in the land was acquired; (5) the immediate and pending use for which the land or the interest in the land was acquired and the status of the land's development for the purpose other than farming; and (6) the present use of the land. Ibid., § 567.8. Failure to register or to file a report as required by this act shall be punishable, for each offense, by a fine of not more than $2,000. Ibid., § 567.11.

Corporate restrictions. No corporation or trust shall either directly or indirectly acquire or otherwise obtain or lease any agricultural land in the state. Iowa Code Ann. § 172C.4 (West supp. 1980–81).

There are several exceptions to this restriction, including those for family-farm corporations and corporations acquiring land for nonagricultural purposes. H.F. 451, Acts of 68th Iowa General Assembly (1979).

Corporations and limited partnerships owning or leasing agricultural land or engaged in farming must file yearly reports with the secretary of state. The corporate reports must include, among other things, the name, address, residence, citizenship of, and number of shares held by any nonresident-alien shareholder holding 5 percent or more of any class of stock. The limited partnership reports must include, among other things, the name, address, residence, and citizenship of each nonresident alien partner. Iowa Code Ann. §§ 172C.5, 172C.6 (supp. 1978–79).

Foreign corporations must obtain a certificate of authority prior to transacting business in this state (model code disclosures). Iowa Code Ann. § 496A.103 (supp. 1979–80).

All corporations must file annual reports (minimal disclosures). Ibid., § 496.1 (supp. 1979–80).

Kansas

Aliens—General restrictions. Aliens ineligible for U.S. citizenship may inherit, hold, or transmit real estate in Kansas only as permitted by treaty. Kan. Stat. Ann. § 59-511 (1976).

The devise of real estate in Kansas is prohibited to any foreign country or subdivision thereof, or city, body politic, or corporation located therein or existing under the laws thereof, except devisees to institutions for religious, educational or charitable purposes. Ibid., § 59-602.

Aliens—Reporting requirements. None.

Corporate restrictions. No corporation, trust, limited corporate partnership, or corporate partnership, shall either directly or indirectly acquire or otherwise obtain or lease any agricultural land in the state. 1981 Kan. Sess. Laws, ch. 106, § 2.

Exceptions to these restrictions are as follows.

1. Family-farm corporations, authorized farm corporations, family trusts, authorized trusts, and testamentary trusts

2. A bona fide encumbrance taken for security
3. Land acquired as a gift, either by grant or devise, by an educational, religious, or charitable nonprofit corporation
4. Land acquired by a corporation which is necessary for the operation of a nonfarming business. Such land may not be used for farming except under lease to a person or entity that is permitted to own or lease agricultural land. The corporation shall not engage in the farming operation nor receive any financial consideration other than rent from the operation
5. Land acquired by a corporation in the collection of debts or through enforcement of a lien
6. A municipal corporation
7. Land acquired by a trust company or bank in a fiduciary capacity for a nonprofit corporation
8. Land owned or leased on July 1, 1981, if the entity owned or leased such land before July 1, 1965; if the entity was in compliance with Kan. Stat. § 17-5901 prior to its repeal by this act; or if the entity was not in compliance with Kan. Stat. § 17-5901 but is in compliance with this act by July 1, 1991
9. Land held or leased by a corporation for use as a feedlot
10. Land used for educational research or scientific or experimental farming
11. Land used for the commerical production of seed for sale or for the growing of alfalfa, by an alfalfa processing entity, if such land is located within thirty miles of such entity's plant site
12. Land owned or leased by a corporate partnership or limited corporate partnership in which the partners therein are persons or entities permitted to own agricultural land
13. Any corporation organized for coal mining purposes that engages in farming on any tract of land owned by it which has been strip mined for coal. 1981 KS. Sess. Laws, ch. 106, § 2.

The attorney general shall institute suits to enforce the provisions of the act. Violators of the act are subject to a civil penalty of not more than $50,000 and must divest themselves of the acquired land within one year. Ibid.

Kentucky

Aliens—General restrictions. Any aliens, not enemies of the United States, after declaring their intentions to become U.S. citizens, may inherit, hold, and alienate real property as if they were citizens. Ky. Rev. Stat. § 381.290 (1972). Realty of an alien may be escheated to the state any time after the expiration of eight years after the acquisition of title, unless the alien disposes of the property or becomes a citizen prior to escheat. Ibid., § 381.300 (1972). The escheat provisions do not apply to corporations even where wholly owned by a nonresident alien. Ibid., § 381.300 (supp. 1978). A resident alien not an enemy may take and hold real property for the purpose of business or residence, for a term not to exceed twenty-one years. Ibid., § 381.320 (1972). Nonresident aliens may hold property acquired by devise or descent for eight years. Ibid., § 381.330.

Aliens—Reporting requirements. None. Note: the Commissioner of Agriculture is required to submit a comprehensive annual report to the Legislative Research Commission, based on information received from the U.S. Secretary of Agriculture under the Agricultural Foreign Investment Disclosure Act of 1978. The report shall contain the names of foreign investors owning land in the Commonwealth of Kentucky, the county in which the land is located, and the number of acres owned by that person. Ky. Rev. Stat. § 246.105 (1980).

Corporate restrictions. No corporation shall hold any real estate except that which is necessary and proper for carrying out its legitimate business, for a period of more than five years (upon penalty of escheat). Ky. Rev. Stat. § 271A.705 (supp. 1981).

Foreign corporations must obtain a certificate of authority in order to transact business within the state (model code disclosures). Ibid., § 271A.520 (supp. 1978).

All corporations must file annual reports (model code disclosures). Ibid., § 271A.615 (supp. 1978).

Louisiana

Aliens—General restrictions. None.

Aliens—Reporting requirements. None.

Corporate restrictions. Foreign corporations must obtain a certificate of authority prior to transacting business in the state (model code disclosures). La. Rev. Stat. Ann. §§ 12:301, 12:304 (West 1969).

All corporations must file annual reports (model code disclosures). Ibid., §§ 12:309, 12:102 (1969).

Maine

Aliens—General restrictions. None.

Aliens—Reporting requirements. None.

Corporate restrictions. Foreign corporations must obtain a certificate of authority prior to transacting business in the state (model code disclosures). Me. Rev. Stat. Ann. tit. 13-A, § 1202 (1977).

All corporations must file annual reports (model code disclosures). Ibid., § 1301 (1977).

Maryland

Aliens—General restrictions. Any alien, not an enemy, may own, sell, devise, dispose of, and otherwise deal with real property in the same manner as if he or she had been a citizen of the state by birth. Md. Real Prop. Code Ann., § 14-101 (1974).

Aliens—Reporting requirements. None.

Corporate restrictions. Foreign corporations must register prior to doing business in the state. All corporations must file annual reports (minimal disclosures). Md. Corps. and Ass'ns Code Ann. §§ 7-202 and 2-314 (supp. 1978).

Massachusetts

Aliens—General restrictions. None.

Aliens—Reporting requirements. None.

Corporate restrictions. Foreign corporations must apply for a certificate of authority within ten days after commencing business in the state (model code disclosures). Mass. Gen. Laws Ann. ch. 181, § 4 (1977). All corporations must file annual reports (model code disclosures). Ibid., ch. 156B, § 109 (supp. 1978).

Michigan

Aliens—General restrictions. None.

Aliens—Reporting requirements. None.

Corporate restrictions. Foreign corporations must obtain a certificate of authority prior to transacting business in the state (model code disclosures). Mich. Stat. Ann. §§ 21.200 (1011), 21.200 (1015) (supp. 1978).

All corporations must file annual reports (model code disclosures). Ibid., §§ 21.100 (901), 21.200 (1003) (1974).

Minnesota

Aliens—General restrictions. No individual shall acquire, directly or indirectly, any interest (including leases) in agricultural land unless the individual is a U.S. citizen or a permanent resident alien. In addition to the restrictions on corporations listed below, no corporation, partnership, trustee, or other business entity shall acquire or obtain any interest in any title to agricultural land unless at least 80 percent of each class of stock is held directly or indirectly by U.S. citizens or permanent resident aliens. Minn. Stat. Ann. § 500.221(2) (West supp. 1981).

Any persons or business entities that acquire an interest in agricultural land after May 27, 1981, and thereafter change status so as to become unqualified to acquire such land must divest themselves of such land within one year of the change in status. A report must also be filed. Ibid.

The exceptions are:

1. Agricultural land acquired by devise or inheritance, as security for indebtedness, in the collection of debts, or enforcement of a lien. However, lands acquired in the collection of debts or by enforcement of a lien must be disposed of within three years of acquisition.
2. The restriction does not apply to citizens of foreign countries whose rights to hold land are secured by treaty.
3. Land used for transportation purposes by a common carrier.
4. Lands acquired for mining purposes. However, pending the mining use, the land may not be used for farming except under lease to a person or entity permitted to hold the land.
5. Lands operated for research or experimental purposes, if the ownership of the land is incidental to the research or experimental objectives and the total acreage owned does not exceed the amount owned on May 27, 1977. Minn. Stat. Ann. § 500.221(2) (West Supp. 1981).

If, after investigation, the commissioner of agriculture has reason to believe that any person is violating this act, he or she shall commence an action in the district court in which the land is located. If a violation is found, the land must be divested within one year. Any land not divested will be sold at public auction. Ibid., § 500.221(3).

Aliens—Reporting requirements. Any natural person, corporation, partnership, trustee, or other business entity prohibited from future acquisition of agricultural land may retain title to any agricultural land lawfully acquired prior to June 1, 1981, but shall file reports with the commissioner of agriculture before January 31 of each year containing the following: description of all agricultural land held within the state; purchase price and market value of the land; the use to which the land is put; date of acquisition; and other reasonable information required by the commissioner. Ibid., § 500.221(4).

Willful failure to properly register any land as required is a gross misdemeanor. Each full month of failure to register is a separate offense. Ibid., § 500.221(5).

Every permanent resident alien who owns property subject to the restrictions above shall annually, sometime in January, file with the commissioner a statement giving the dates and places of that person's residence in the United States during the prior calendar year. The statement must include an explanation of any absences totaling more than six months and any facts that support the continuation of permanent resident alien status. The commissioner shall review the statement within thirty days and notify the alien whether the facts support continuation of the permanent resident status. Ibid., § 500.221(1a).

Corporate restrictions. No corporation or pension or investment fund shall engage in farming, nor directly or indirectly own, acquire, or otherwise obtain any interest in any land used or capable of being used for farming. Minn. Stat. Ann. § 500.24(3) (West supp. 1981).

There are a number of exceptions to this restriction for family farms, experimental farms, breeding farms, nonprofit corporations, and land acquired as a gift. Ibid., § 500.24(3).

Foreign corporations must obtain a certificate of authority prior to transacting business in the state (model code disclosures). Ibid., §§ 303.03, 303.06 (1969).

Foreign corporations must file an annual report (model code disclosures). Ibid., § 303.14 (1969).

Mississippi

Aliens—General restrictions. Resident aliens may hold and dispose of land as if they were citizens. Nonresident aliens may not own land, upon penalty of escheat, with the following exceptions: persons who have declared their intentions to become citizens, property acquired as security for a debt, and citizens of Syria and Lebanon acquiring through inheritance. Nonresident aliens may also acquire land through enforcement of a lien but may not hold the land for more than twenty years. Miss. Code Ann. § 89-1-23 (1974).

Aliens-Reporting requirements. None.

Corporate restrictions. Corporations, nonresident aliens, and associations composed in whole or in part by nonresident aliens may not directly or indirectly purchase or become owners of state land. Miss. Code Ann. § 29-1-75 (1972).

Foreign corporations must obtain a certificate of authority prior to transacting business in the state (model code disclosures). Ibid., §§ 79-3-211, 79-3-219 (1972).

All corporations must file annual reports (model code disclosures). Ibid., § 79-3-249 (supp. 1978).

Missouri

Aliens—General restrictions. No nonresident alien, foreign business, or agent, trustee, or fiduciary thereof shall acquire by grant, purchase, devise, descent or otherwise agricultural land in the state. Leases and options for terms of ten years or longer are included in this restriction. Mo. Ann. Stat. §§ 442.571, 442.581 (Vernon supp. 1981).

Any resident aliens who cease to be bona fide residents of the United States shall divest themselves of their agricultural lands within two years. Any agricultural lands not divested within two years will be ordered sold at public sale. Ibid., 442.586.

The exceptions are:

1. agricultural land owned before August 13, 1978, so long as it is held by the same owner.
2. agricultural land or any interest therein acquired for the immediate or potential use in nonfarming purposes. This land may be held in such acreage as may be necessary to the nonfarm business operation. However, pending the development for the nonfarm purpose, the land may not be used for farming except under lease to certain entities permitted by statute. Ibid., § 442.591.

If land is acquired in violation of the act or ceases to be used for nonfarming purposes, the attorney general shall bring an action in the circuit court of the county where the land is located. When a violation is found, the court shall order that the land be divested within two years. Any land not divested within two years will be sold at public sale. Ibid., § 442.576.

Aliens—Reporting requirements. Any foreign person who held any interest (including leases of ten years or more and beneficial interests in land under contracts of sale), other than a security interest, in agricultural land on September 28, 1979, should have submitted a report to the director of agriculture within sixty days of that date. Those reports already submitted and those reports filed late must contain the following:

1. The legal name and address of the foreign entity.
2. The citizenship of the foreign entity or its principal place of business and nation where it was created.
3. The legal name and address of each person who holds a substantial interest in the foreign entity and that entity's citizenship or its principal place of business and the nation where it was created.
4. The type of interest that is held in agricultural land.
5. A legal description of the agricultural land, including the total acreage involved.
6. The date of acquisition and purchase price.
7. A declaration of the agricultural use.
8. If the land was acquired for a nonfarm use, its intended use. Ibid., § 442.592.

Any foreign person who acquires or transfers any interest, other than a security interest, in agricultural land, must submit a report to the director of agriculture within thirty days of such acquisition or transfer. The report must contain the same information as listed above, plus, if the land is transferred, the name, address, and citizenship or principal place of business of the person to whom the land was transferred. Ibid.

Any person who fails to file a report required under the provisions of this section is liable for an amount not to exceed 25 percent of the fair market value of the person's interest in the agricultural land. Ibid.

Corporate restrictions. Alien corporations are specifically authorized to acquire, own, hold, and alienate "real estate except agricultural land." Ibid., § 442.560(1) (1978).

A foreign business, defined as any business entity, regardless of form, in which a controlling interest is owned by aliens, is prohibited from acquiring "agricultural land" after the effective date of the statute (August 13, 1978) and must divest any such land within ten years. Ibid., § 442.560(4). Corporate ownership of agricultural land is generally prohibited with the major exceptions of family-farm corporations and corporations owning agricultural land as of September 18, 1975. Ibid., § 492.560 (supp. 1979).

The attorney general shall institute an action in county circuit court for suspected violations. If the court finds a violation, it shall order that the land be divested within two years. Any lands not divested within such time shall be ordered sold at public sale. Ibid., § 350.030.

Every corporation engaged in farming or proposing to commence farming must file a report with the director of agriculture. No corporation may commence farming in the state until it has filed the report. The report must contain the following:

1. The name and place of incorporation of the corporation.
2. The name and address of the registered office in the state and the name and address of the registered agent.
3. The acreage and location of land owned or leased for farming.
4. The names and addresses of officers and directors of the corporation. Ibid., § 350.020.

A corporation seeking to qualify as a family-farm corporation or an authorized farm corporation must report the following additional information:

1. The number of shares owned by persons residing on the farm or actively engaged in farming, or their relatives.
2. The name, address, and number of shares owned by each shareholder.

3. The percentage of net receipts derived from sources other than farming. Ibid.

Every corporation engaged in farming in the state, except a family-farm corporation, shall file reports such as those listed above, whenever any of the initially filed information changes; whenever the ownership of the controlling interest in the corporation changes; or whenever the land ceases to be used for farming or is sold. Ibid.

Failure to file a required report or the use of false information shall be a misdemeanor punishable by a fine of not less than $500 or more than $1,000. Ibid.

Montana

Aliens—General restrictions. An alien's right to inherit and devise realty is contingent upon reciprocal rights in the alien's home country for U.S. citizens. Mont. Code Ann. § 91A-2-11 (supp. 1977).

State lands may be sold only to citizens and those persons who have declared their intent to become citizens or corporations organized under the laws of this state. No person or corporation is eligible to purchase more than one section of land, and this area shall not include more than 160 acres of land susceptible of irrigation. Ibid., §§ 77-2-306, 77-2-307.

Aliens—Reporting requirements. None.

Corporate restrictions. Foreign corporations must obtain a certificate of authority prior to transacting business in the state (model code disclosures). Ibid., §§ 15-22-99, 15-22-103 (1967 and supp. 1967).

All corporations must file an annual report (model code disclosures and the value of all property within the state). Ibid., § 15-22-118 (1967).

Nebraska

Aliens—General restrictions. Aliens are prohibited from acquiring title to or holding interests in land except within the corporate limits of a city or village or within three miles thereof, and leases on any land for more than five years from the date of acquisition (under penalty of escheat). Neb. Rev. Stat. § 76-414 (1976).

A resident alien may acquire land by devise or descent only, provided the alien disposes of the property within five years from the date of acquisition (under penalty of escheat). Ibid., § 76-405 (1976).

A nonresident alien's right of inheritance is contingent upon a reciprocal right for U.S. citizens in the alien's home country. Ibid., § 4-107 (1977).

Aliens—Reporting requirements: see corporate restrictions.

Corporate restrictions. No corporation or syndicate shall acquire or otherwise obtain an interest, whether legal, beneficial, or otherwise, in any title to real estate used for farming or ranching in this state, or engage in farming or ranching. Neb. Const., Art. 12, Sec. 8(1).

There are a number of exceptions to this restriction, including family trusts, land acquired for nonfarming purposes, American Indians, encumbrances for security, and land acquired for research or experimental purposes.

The secretary of state monitors corporate and syndicate purchase of farming and ranching lands, and reports possible violations of the above law to the attorney general. Any land held in violation of the state constitution must be divested within two years or be escheated to the state.

Note: When the above-listed restrictions were enacted by constitutional amendment in November 1982, the state legislature rescinded all existing reporting requirements for corporations.

Nevada

Aliens—General restrictions. A nonresident alien's right to take by will or descent is dependent upon a reciprocal right in the alien's country to take and receive payment. Nev. Rev. Stat. § 134.230 (1977).

Aliens—Reporting requirements. None.

Corporate requirements. Foreign corporations must obtain a certificate of authority prior to transacting business in the state (model code disclosures). Ibid., § 80.010 (1977).

All corporations must file annual reports (model code disclosures). Ibid., § 80.110 (1977).

New Hampshire

Aliens—General restrictions. An alien resident in this state may take, purchase, hold, convey or devise real estate; and it may descend in the same manner as for citizens. N.H. Rev. Stat. Ann. § 477.20 (1968). This has been taken to mean that nonresident aliens may not inherit property. *Hanglin* v. *McCarthy,* 95 N.H. 36, 37, 57A. 2d 148, 149 (1948); *Lazaron* v. *Morares,* 101 N.H. 383, 143A. 2d 669 (1958).

Aliens—Reporting requirements. None.

Corporate restrictions. Foreign corporations must obtain a certificate of authority prior to transacting business in this state (model code disclosures). N.H. Rev. Stat. Ann. § 300.4 (1977).

All corporations must file annual reports (model code disclosures). Ibid., § 294.105 (1977).

New Jersey

Aliens—General restrictions. None.

Aliens—Reporting requirements. None.

Corporate restrictions. Foreign corporations must obtain a certificate of authority prior to transacting business in this state (model code disclosures). N.J. Stat. Ann. §§ 14A:13-3, 14A:13-4 (West 1969).

All corporations must file annual reports (model code disclosures). Ibid., § 14A:4-5 (supp. 1978, 1978).

Foreign corporations that are not doing business in the state (and thus disclaim need for certification of authority), but which have certain "minimal" contacts within the state, must file a business activities report supplied by the state. Minimal contacts include ownership of real property. Ibid., §§ 14A:13-15 (supp. 1978–79).

New Mexico

Aliens—General restrictions. None.

Aliens—Reporting requirements. None.

Corporate restrictions. Foreign corporations must obtain a certificate of authority prior to transacting business in the state (model code disclosures and an estimate of value of all property to be owned in the state in the current fiscal year). N.M. Stat. Ann. §§ 53-17-1, 53-17-5 (1978).

All corporations must make annual reports (model code disclosures). Ibid., § 53-5-2 (1978).

New York

Aliens—General Restrictions. None.

Aliens—Reporting requirements. None.

Corporate restrictions. Foreign corporations must have a certificate of authority prior to transacting business in the state. N.Y. Bus. Corp. Law § 1304 (1963 and supp. 1978–79).

North Carolina

Aliens—General restrictions. The right of nonresident aliens to inherit real property is contingent on the reciprocal right existing in the alien's home country for U.S. citizens. The burden is on the nonresident alien to establish the existence of a reciprocal right. In the absence of reciprocity, the property will be disposed of as escheated property. N.C. Gen. Stat. §§ 64-3, 64-4, 64-5 (1975).

Aliens—Reporting requirements. The secretary of state is authorized and directed to collect all information obtainable from reports by aliens made to agencies of the federal government on ownership of real property interests in North Carolina, to be updated every three months, and to maintain a file on such information that shall be available to members of the General Assembly and the public. Ibid., § 64-1.1 (1979).

Corporate restrictions. Foreign corporations must obtain a certificate of authority prior to transacting business in the state (model code disclosures). Ibid., § 55-140 (1975).

North Dakota

Aliens—General restrictions. A person who is not a U.S. citizen, except a permanent resident alien or a citizen of Canada, may not acquire, directly or indirectly, any interest (including leasehold interests) in agricultural land. Nor may a partnership, limited partnership, trustee, or other business entity, directly or indirectly, acquire or otherwise obtain any interest (including leasehold interests) in any title to agricultural land, unless the ultimate beneficial interest of the entity is held directly or indirectly by U.S. citizens or permanent resident aliens. N.D. Cent. Code § 47-10.1-02 (supp. 1979), as amended by 1981 N.D. Sess. Laws ch. 460, effective April 3, 1981.

Exceptions include the following:

1. land acquired by devise or inheritance, as security for indebtedness, in the collection of debts, or by enforcement of a lien. However, land acquired in the collection of debts or by enforcement of a lien shall be disposed of within three years of acquiring such ownership, if the acquisition would otherwise be a violation;
2. a foreign corporation may acquire agricultural land for use as an industrial site where construction contracts are entered into by the corporation within 150 days after acquisition of the land. Only so much land as is necessary for industrial purposes may be acquired, and the land may be held only so long as it is used for industrial purposes. The land must be disposed of within one year after acquisition if construction contracts are not entered into within 150 days after acquisition;
3. citizens or subjects of a foreign country whose rights to hold land are secured by treaty and railroad common carriers are not subject to the restrictions;
4. land acquired prior to July 1, 1979. Ibid.

The attorney general shall enforce these provisions by filing an action in the district court of the county where any land held in violation of this act is situated. If the court finds the land in question is held in violation of this act, it shall enter an order so declaring. The person or business entity holding the land shall then have one year to divest itself of the land. Any land not divested within one year shall be sold at public sale. N.D. Cent. Code § 47-10.1-04 (supp. 1979).

Aliens—Reporting requirements. Any individual, partnership, limited partnership, trustee, or other business entity prohibited from future acquisition of agricultural land should have submitted a report to the commissioner of agriculture by October 1, 1979, for any land acquired before July 1, 1979. Reports by such individuals or entities are also required before July 1 of each year, and the commissioner shall make the information available to the public. The reports should contain the following:

1. a description of all agricultural land owned within the state;
2. the purchase price and market value of the land;
3. the use to which the land is put;
4. the date of acquisition; and
5. any other reasonable information the commissioner may require. Ibid., § 47-10.1-05.

Corporate restrictions. All corporations (including joint stock companies or associations) are prohibited from owning or leasing land used for farming or ranching and from engaging in the business of farming or ranching. N.D. Cent. Code § 10-06-01.

The attorney general or any resident of the county may commence an action in the district court where the land is located, for suspected violations of the act. If the court finds a violation, the corporation must divest itself of the land and cease all farming and ranching operations within one year. Any corporation that fails to comply with the court's order shall be dissolved by the secretary of state. Any land not divested with one year will be sold at public sale. Ibid., §§ 10, 11 (§§ 10-06-13, 10-06-14).

Every corporation engaged in farming or ranching after June 30, 1981, shall file a report with the secretary of state at the time of the filing of the corporation's articles of incorporation, and thereafter annually prior to April 15. Information from the reports will be printed in a newspaper in each county where land is owned or leased by a corporation filing a report. No corporation may commence farming or ranching in the state until the secretary of state has certified the initial report. The reports must contain the following:

1. the name of the corporation and its place of incorporation;
2. the address of the registered office and the name and address of the registered agent in the state;
3. the acreage and location of all land owned or leased in the state and used for farming or ranching;
4. the names and addresses of the officers and directors;
5. the number of shares of stock or the percentage of interest in the acreage corporation used for farming or ranching, that is owned

or leased by persons residing on the farm or ranch and actively engaged in farming or ranching, or by relatives;

6. the name, address, relationship, and number of shares of stock or percentage of interest in the acreage the corporation used for farming or ranching, which is owned or leased by each shareholder or beneficiary; and

7. The percentage of gross receipts derived from rent, royalties, dividends, interest, and annuities. Ibid., § 5 (§ 10-06-08).

Every corporation that fails to file a required report or willfully files false information is guilty of a misdemeanor. Ibid., §§ 5, 6 (§§ 10-06-08, 10-06-09).

Foreign corporations must obtain a certificate of authority prior to transacting business in the state (model code disclosures and an estimate of the value of property to be located in the state). Ibid., §§ 10-22-01, 10-22-05 (1976).

All corporations must file an annual report (model code disclosures). Ibid., § 10-23-01 (1976).

Ohio

Aliens—General restrictions. None.

Aliens—Reporting requirements. All nonresident aliens who acquire any interest, directly or indirectly, in real property located in this state that is in excess of three acres or that has a market value greater than $100,000, or any interest in mining or minerals that has a market value in excess of $50,000 shall, within thirty days of the acquisition, file a report with the secretary of state. The report shall contain the following:

1. name, address, and telephone number;
2. country of citizenship;
3. location and amount of acreage of real property; and
4. Intended use of real property at time of filing. Ohio Rev. Code Ann. § 5301.254(B) (page 1981).

Nonresident aliens or business entities that acquired real property prior to the effective date of this act, and who otherwise would have been subject to its provisions, must file reports within one year after the effective date of this act (March 19, 1979). Ibid., § 5301.99 (page 1979).

Persons or entities required to report their acquisitions under the act shall also report the sale of the property or any change in their status within thirty days of the sale or change in status. Ibid., § 5301.254(D).

Any individual, corporation, or business entity that violates the act will be fined not less than $5,000 nor more than an amount equal to 25 percent of the market value of the property. Ibid., §§ 5301.99.

Corporate restrictions. Corporations and other business entities must also file reports if they acquire any interest in real property that exceeds the limits stated above, and if either a nonresident alien owns at least a 10-percent interest in the real entity or any number of nonresident aliens own at least a 40-percent interest in the entity. The reports must be made within thirty days of acquisition and contain the following information:

1. name, address of principal place of business, and address of principal Ohio office;
2. name, address, telephone number, and country of citizenship of each nonresident alien who owns at least a 10-percent interest in the entity;
3. location and amount of acreage of real property;
4. principal business of corporation or entity;
5. intended use of real property at time of filing;
6. name of the chairman of governing board (if any), chief executive (if any), and partners (if any);
7. name of the corporation's or entity's agent in the state;
8. place of incorporation, if a corporation; and
9. number of persons who own shares of stock or other interests. Ibid., § 5301.254 (1979).

Foreign corporations must obtain a license to do business prior to transacting business in the state (model code disclosures). Ohio Rev. Code §§ 1703.03, 1703.04 (1978).

All corporations must file annual reports (model code disclosures and location of property used by the corporation within the state). Ibid., § 1703.07 (1978).

Oklahoma

Aliens—General restrictions. The state constitution declares that aliens who are not United States citizens or bona fide Oklahoma residents are prohibited from acquiring or owning land. Alien nonresidents who acquire land by devise, descent, or purchase, where such purchase is made under foreclosure liens, may hold the land but must dispose of it within five years of acquiring title, upon penalty of escheat. In addition, resident aliens who cease to be bona fide residents must dispose of their land within five years of ceasing to be residents. Okla. Const. Art. 22, Sec. 1, Okla. Stat. Ann. tit. 60, §§ 121–124 (West 1971).

Aliens—Reporting requirements. None.

Corporate restrictions. The Oklahoma supreme court has held that restrictions on alien landownership apply to alien corporations. However, an alien corporation licensed to do business in Oklahoma is considered a resident of the state and is not subject to the restrictions listed above. Okla. Sup. Ct., 630 P.2d 1253 (1981).

Corporations are prohibited from engaging in farming, with a few limited exceptions (such as family corporations). Foreign corporations must be domesticated before transacting business in the state (model code disclosures and an estimate of the value of the property to be located within the state in the current fiscal year). No corporation shall own real estate outside any incorporated city or town except as such real estate is necessary and proper for carrying on the business for which the corporation has been lawfully incorporated or domesticated in this state. Ibid., tit. 18, §§ 951, 1.199, 1.228, 1.20 (supp. 1978–79).

Oregon

Aliens—General restrictions. Only citizens and persons who have declared their intention to become citizens may purchase state lands. Or. Rev. Stat. § 273.255 (1977).

Aliens—Reporting requirements. None.

Corporate restrictions. Foreign corporations must obtain a certificate of authority prior to doing business in the state (model code disclosures). Ibid., § 57.675.

All corporations must file annual reports (model code disclosures). Ibid., § 57.755.

All corporations that conduct any farming or that own or lease any farmland must file additional disclosures that include, among other things, name and business address of each entity that controls 10 percent or more of the voting shares of the corporation, and the name of the county in which it leases or owns more than 40 acres of farmland, or where it conducts farming operations. Ibid., § 57.757 (1977).

Pennsylvania

Aliens—General restrictions. An alien who is not a resident of a state or territory of the United States or of the District of Columbia, and a foreign government shall not acquire an interest in agricultural land exceeding one hundred acres, except as such interest may be acquired by devise or inheritance, as may be held as security for indebtedness, or as is permitted by treaty. 68 Pa. Stat. Ann. § 41 (Purdon supp. 1981–82).

Aliens—Reporting requirements. None.

Corporate restrictions. Foreign corporations must obtain a certificate of authority prior to transacting business in the state (model code disclosures). Pa. Stat. Ann. tit. 15, §§ 2004 (Purdon supp. 1978–79).

Rhode Island

Aliens—General restrictions. None.

Aliens—Reporting requirements. None.

Corporate restrictions. Foreign corporations must obtain a certificate of authority prior to transacting business in the state (model code disclosures and an estimate of the value of property to be owned in the state in the following year). R.I. Gen. Laws §§ 7-1.1-100, 7-1.1-103 (1970 and supp. 1977).

All corporations must file annual reports (model code disclosures). Ibid., §§ 7-1.1-118, (1970 and supp. 1977).

South Carolina

Aliens—General restrictions. Aliens and corporations controlled by aliens may not own or control more than 500,000 acres of land within the state. Lands acquired through the foreclosures of mortgages are excluded, provided the excess lands are disposed of within five years. S.C. Code Ann. §§ 27-13-30, 27-13-40 (Law Co-op. 1976).

Aliens—Reporting requirements. None.

Corporate restrictions. Foreign corporations must obtain a certificate of authority prior to transacting business in the state (model code disclosures). Ibid., §§ 33-23-20 (1976).

South Dakota

Aliens—General restrictions. No alien who is not a resident of this state, of some state or territory of the United States or of the District of Columbia, and no foreign government shall hereafter acquire agricultural lands, or any interest therein, exceeding 160 acres, except such as may be acquired through devise or inheritance, and such as may be held as security for indebtedness. The provisions of this section do not apply to citizens, foreign governments, or subjects of a foreign country whose right to hold land is secure by treaty. S.D. Compiled Laws Ann. § 43-2A-2 (supp. 1980).

All nonresident aliens who may acquire agricultural lands in this state by devise or descent shall have three years from the date of so acquiring such title in which to alienate such agricultural lands. Ibid., § 43—2A-5.

All agricultural lands acquired or held in violation of §§ 43—2A-2 and 43-2A-3 shall be forfeited to the state. Ibid., § 43-2A-6.

Aliens—Reporting requirements. None. Note: The state department of agriculture shall monitor, for compliance to this chapter, biannual reports transmitted to the department pursuant to section 6 of the United States Agricultural Foreign Investment Disclosure Act of 1978. Ibid., §§ 43-2A-6, 43-2A-7 (1979).

Corporate restrictions. Foreign corporations must obtain a certificate of authority prior to transacting business in the state (model code disclosures and an estimate of the value of property within the state to be owned by the corporation during the following year). S.D. Compiled Laws Ann. § 47-8-7 (1967).

All corporations must file an annual report (disclosures nearly identical to those listed under reporting requirements). Ibid., § 47-9-1 (1967).

No corporation shall engage in farming, nor shall any corporation own or acquire agricultural land. Ibid., § 47-9A-3 (supp. 1980).

There are a number of exceptions to this restrictions; see Ibid., §§ 47-9A-4, 47-9A-5, 47-9A-6, 47-9A-7, 47-9A-8, 47-9A-9, 47-9A-11, 47-9A-12, and 47-9A-13.

Tennessee

Aliens—General restrictions. None.

Aliens—Reporting requirements. None.

Corporate restrictions. Foreign corporations must obtain a certificate of authority prior to transacting business in the state (model code disclosures). Tenn. Code Ann. § 48-11-3 (supp. 1977).

Texas

Aliens—General restrictions. None.

Aliens—Reporting requirements. None.

Corporate restrictions. All restrictions regarding corporate ownership of Texas farmland have been repealed by the 1983 legislature. See Texas Rev. Civ. Stat. ann., art. 1302, §§ 4.01–4.07 (1983).

Utah

Aliens—General restrictions. None.

Aliens—Reporting requirements. None.

Corporate restrictions. Foreign corporations must obtain a certificate of authority prior to transacting business in the state (model code disclosures and an estimate of the value of the property to be owned within the state in the following year). Utah Code Ann. § 16-10-106 (1973).

All corporations must file an annual report (disclosures nearly the same as in previous paragraph). Ibid., § 16-10-121 (1973).

Vermont

Aliens—General restrictions. The right to acquire, hold, and transfer land is granted by the Vermont constitution to persons who settle in the state who have taken the oath of allegiance. Vt. Const. ch. 2, § 62.

Aliens—Reporting requirements. None.

Corporate restrictions. Foreign corporations must obtain a certificate of authority prior to transacting business in the state (model code disclosures). Vt. Stat. Ann. tit. 11, § 2105 (1973).

All corporations must file annual reports (model code disclosure). Ibid., § 2151 (1973).

Virginia

Aliens—General restrictions. Any alien not an enemy may acquire, inherit, hold, and transmit real estate the same as U.S. citizens. Va. Code § 55-1 (1974).

Aliens—Reporting requirements. Virginia has passed legislation entitled "Foreign Agricultural Investment Disclosure Act" which has reporting requirements similar to the federal Public Law 95-460 (AFIDA). Va. Code §§ 3.1-22.22–3.1-22.27 (supp. 1980). The Virginia Commissioner of Agriculture has decided not to implement requirements and relies solely on AFIDA data received through the U.S. Department of Agriculture.

Corporate restrictions. Foreign corporations must obtain a certificate of authority prior to transacting business in the state (model code disclosures). Va. Code §§ 13.1-102, 13.1-106 (1978).

All corporations must file annual reports (model code disclosures). Ibid., § 13.1-120 (1978).

Washington

Aliens—General restrictions. None.

Aliens—Reporting requirements. None.

Corporate restrictions. Foreign corporations must obtain a certificate of authority prior to transacting business in the state (model code disclosures). Wash. Rev. Code Ann. §§ 23A.32.010, 23A.32.050 (1969 and supp. 1977).

West Virginia

Aliens—General restrictions. None.

Aliens—Reporting requirements. None.

Corporate restrictions. Corporations holding more than 10,000 acres of land within the state must pay a yearly tax of 5 cents per acre on the land in excess of 10,000 acres. W. Va. Code § 11-12-75.

Foreign corporations must pay a higher license tax than domestic corporations. The tax assessment is based on the amount of property owned within the state, and foreign corporations must file a report (separate from the annual report) disclosing the amount of property owned within the state. Ibid., §§ 11-12-80, 11-12-81 (supp. 1980).

Foreign corporations must obtain a certificate of authority prior to transacting business in the state (model code disclosures). Ibid., §§ 31-1-49, 31-1-53 (1975).

All corporations must file annual reports (model code disclosures and where property owned within the state is situated, of what it consists, and the number of acres). Ibid., § 31-1-56a.

Wisconsin

Aliens—General restrictions. An alien who is not a resident of some state or territory of the United States or of the District of Columbia cannot acquire or hold more than 640 acres, except by devise or descent, or pursuant to the collection of debt. The penalty is forfeiture to the state. Ibid., § 710.02 (Spec. Pamphlet 1980).

Aliens—Reporting requirements. None.

Corporate restrictions. A corporation not incorporated within the United States or a corporation of which more than 20 percent of the stock is owned by nonresident aliens is prohibited from holding more than 640 acres of land, unless such land was acquired through inheritance or upon a debt (upon penalty of escheat). Ibid., §§ 710.01, 710.02, 710.03.

No corporation may own land on which to carry out farming operations. Ibid., § 182.001(1) (supp. 1980–81).

Foreign corporations must obtain a certificate of authority prior to transacting business in the state (model code disclosures). Ibid., §§ 180.801, 180.813 (1957 and supp. 1978–79).

All corporations must file an annual report (model code disclosures). Ibid., §§ 180.791 (1957 and supp. 1978–79).

Wyoming

Aliens—General restrictions. Nonresident aliens not eligible for citizenship under the laws of the United States are prohibited from acquiring, posessing, enjoying, using, leasing, transferring, transmitting, or inheriting real property except to the extent that a reciprocal right exists for U.S. citizens in the alien's country of citizenship. Wyo. Stat. §§ 34-15-101, 34-15-102 (1983). A similar restriction exists with respect to nonresident alien acquisition of real estate by succession. See Wyo. Stat. §§ 2-4-105, 2-4-106 (1980).

Aliens—Reporting requirements. None.

Corporate restrictions. Foreign corporations must obtain a certificate of authority prior to transacting business in the state (model code disclosures and an estimate of the value of the property within the state to be owned in the following year). Ibid, §§ 17-1-701, 17-1-1705 (1977).

All corporations must file annual reports (model code disclosures). Ibid., § 17-2-101 (1977).

Enforcement

Most of the laws restricting foreign ownership or acquisition of U.S. real estate have evolved out of similar legislation passed in the late nineteenth century. These statutes were a result of the strong feeling against foreign landowners that pervaded the country, especially the midwestern farming belt, during the late nineteenth and early twentieth centuries.

The record of enforcement among the states with restrictive statutes is variable. No violations are recorded at all in Illinois, and only a few old cases are reported in New Hampshire. Enforcement efforts have been strictly passive—no state officials have actively sought out violators and penalized them. Enforcement of the law is generally the responsibility of the state's attorney, *when a violation is brought to their attention.* Thus, though most of the attorneys general do not search actively for violators, they will take action if a violation is brought to their attention. Penalties generally range from fines to escheatment of property to the state.

The passage of reporting laws by particular states prior to 1978, and the advent of the AFIDA in that year, provided the states for the first time with information regarding ownership of the land. Although enforcement of legal restrictions against foreign ownership remains passive, violations of the statutes are more easily drawn to the attention of the attorneys general since AFIDA than in the absence of any reporting requirements.

The Agricultural Foreign Investment Disclosure Act (AFIDA) became effective February 2, 1979. The law requires all foreign persons holding agricultural land as of February 1, 1979, to file a report of such holdings by August 1, 1979, with the Secretary of Agriculture. All foreign persons who acquire or dispose of agricultural land on or after February 2, 1979, are required to report such transactions within ninety days of the transfer.

In accordance with the act, completed report forms are transmitted by the Secretary of Agriculture to each state detailing foreign ownership of land in that state, every six months. However, the value of AFIDA, as well as of the state-instituted reporting requirements, is mitigated by the relative ease with which foreign entities can mask involvement in landownership through corporate layering or other legal maneuvering. There is thus reason to suspect that the magnitude of foreign investment in U.S. agricultural real estate is probably understated.

In the sense that *existing* violations may be difficult to uncover, the passage of laws restricting foreign ownership of U.S. farmland have probably had little net impact on the farming community. In a different sense, such regulation probably has affected the *pattern* of foreign acquisition of U.S. farmland by changing the relative price (and thus expected return) of investing in agricultural real estate, as opposed to other types of real estate, and other investments more generally. In certain instances, these marginal changes may prevent potential foreign purchasers from entering the market for U.S. farmland in the first place.

Notes

1. The information for this summary was drawn from four sources: "Foreign Investment in U.S. Real Estate: Report of the Committee on Foreign Investment in U.S. Real Estate," *Real Property, Probate and Trust Journal* Vol. 14:1 (Spring 1979):1–41; R.L. Morse, H.C. Reeves, and N.E. Harl, "State Controls and Reporting Requirements," in *Monitoring Foreign Ownership of U.S. Real Estate,* Vol. 1, USDA (1979); J.W. Mayer, *State Laws Relating to the Ownership of U.S. Land by Aliens and Business Entities,* USDA Staff Report AGES811113 (November 1981); and replies from the secretaries of state and the attorneys general to letters sent to each state requesting an update on the legal status of foreign and corporate participation in the real estate market. Special thanks are due to Mr. Dale Schian from USDA for generously sharing information from a forthcoming USDA study that examines state legal restrictions on foreign and corporate ownership of U.S. farmland.

7 Related Topics

In chapter 4, a rent-seeking model of individual wealth-maximizing behavior by small, family farmers was invoked to explain the pattern of existing legislative restrictions against nonresident alien ownership of U.S. farmland. Two topics that relate directly to that theory are explored in this chapter.

First, a general similarity is noted between Albert Breton's theory of nationalism and the theory presented in chapter 4. Though Breton's theory as such cannot explain the pattern of state restrictions against foreign ownership of U.S. agricultural land, it is capable of explaining some portion of the variation in restrictions imposed by other countries of the world on maintenance of property rights by outsiders, particularly U.S. citizens.

Second, a closer look is taken at the incidence of legislative restrictions on corporate ownership of U.S. farmland. It has been argued previously that small farmers have incentives to restrict the domestic, as well as the foreign, components of the demand for farmland. Why then do corporate restrictions occur in only a handful of states? The answer, of course, hinges on the relative costs of lobbying against domestic versus foreign ownership of U.S. land.

Nationalism as Rent-Seeking Behavior

The model presented in chapter 4, of self-interested small farmers capturing rents in the form of lower farmland prices from the larger farmers via the legislative process, has a familiar ring to it. In essence, it is simply an application of the rent-seeking paradigm that emerged in the late 1960s and early 1970s out of the positive economic inquiry into (or the public-choice approach to) the political process, incited by Buchanan and Tullock's *The Calculus of Consent.*[1]

The specific setting—small, family farmers versus large farmers and real estate interests, with foreigners bearing the brunt of the state regulatory efforts—permits the resultant analysis to compare favorably with Albert Breton's economic theory of nationalism.[2] The former model provides an explanation for state restrictions against foreign nationals with respect to farmland ownership that is fairly robust. The latter theory is able to partially explain the pattern of worldwide restrictions by countries with respect to ownership rights therein by U.S. citizens.

Breton's theory of nationalism is reviewed briefly here, and then his theory of nationalism and the theory of farmland regulation put forward in this book are compared and identified as special cases of rent-seeking behavior. Both theories are put to the test of explaining legal restrictions on property rights that have been implemented by other nations against outsiders, particularly against U.S. citizens.

The Economic Theory of Nationalism: A Review

Breton distinguishes between what he calls cultural nationalism and political nationalism. The former type he dismisses as being of little economic significance. Political nationalism, however, generates behavior that consists of making demands and claims against or on some other national or ethnic group. Justification for these demands and claims is based on the dependency of group identity or survival on the favorable response to these claims by the external group.[3]

The theory itself posits that nationalism is used as a vehicle whereby nationalists redistribute some portion of the stock of wealth located in their political jurisdiction in their own favor. Of course, such wealth redistribution does not come without a price—Breton argues implicitly that nationalism will be utilized as a redistributive mechanism only as long as the marginal returns from so doing outweigh the marginal costs.

Two principal sets of instruments are available to nationalists in their efforts to alter (favorably for themselves) the existing and future distribution of wealth in their territory: nationalization and purchase of foreign-owned assets; and tariffs, taxes, subsidies, and the like, whose ultimate effect is to encourage ownership of assets by domestic citizens (individuals and corporations).

According to Breton, the primary benefit conferred on nationals as a result of their efforts takes the form of high-income jobs for middle-class workers, who have, not coincidentally, a great deal of power in the voting booth. To the extent that ownership of assets is gained through nationalistic behavior, middle-class labor obtains the power to influence the prevailing capital/labor ratio employed in production. The productivity of these factors of production does not determine relative use in production; rather, the mix is determined by considering the productivity of middle-class labor as modified by the ethnic or national origin of the labor factor. The end result is that some subset of the population will be paid more than they are worth because they are members of the so-called proper ethnic or national group. In addition, more people may be employed than is economically efficient.[4]

It is clear that Breton's theory represents one example of a more general phenomenon: that special-interest associations manage to lobby successfully for income protection or enhancing legislation from the government apparatus. The politics of rent-seeking have been investigated widely by public-choice theorists in the 1970s; there is no need to elaborate further upon their work. It is sufficient to say that it is the redistributive motive that underlies efforts by U.S. war veterans, handicapped individuals, minority groups, automobile manufacturers, opticians, truckers, and many other diverse interest groups to lobby in the halls of Washington or the state capitals for special legislation.

The model presented in chapter 4 constitutes another example of the more general phenomenon of special-interest lobbying, in a setting that shares certain similarities with the one investigated by Breton. In particular, restrictions are imposed against foreigners. There are sound economic reasons for doing so, as argued by McCormick and Tollison.[5] They maintain that the least-cost method of obtaining beneficial regulation through the state is to shift the costs of regulation to a group external to their own political jurisdiction. This minimizes the presence of opposing interests which are represented in the same governing body as is the affected group.

With respect to U.S. farmland, foreigners are not in a position to put up an effective resistance to restrictive legislation in the state capitals. In addition, foreigners may be identified fairly readily by farmers or other nationals (via disclosure requirements), which makes the cost of enforcing anti-alien legislation relatively low. In short, it is easy to pick on foreign owners of U.S. agricultural land because the cost of arousing public (and legislative) sympathies against them is low. Even if the expected returns of anti-alien legislation are not great, they may be high enough to justify legislative rent-seeking by small, family farmers.

There is one notable difference between the two models. In Breton's model, nationalists gain high-paying, middle-class jobs as a result of restrictions instituted against foreigners. These jobs come at the expense of the foreigners who held them previously. In the model put forth in chapter 4, gains to small farmers take the form of lower prices paid for farmland. These gains come at the expense not only of foreigners in the market for U.S. farmland, but also of large farmers who are potential suppliers of farmland to aliens, and who realize capital gains that are lower than they would be in the absence of regulation, and of real estate agents who suffer a reduced volume of business. This difference suggests that restrictions against nonresident aliens will be opposed more strongly in the latter case than in the former, and will be more costly to achieve as a result.

Therefore, Breton's economic theory of nationalism cannot be of much assistance in attempting to explain the incidence of state restrictions against foreign ownership of U.S. farmland, even though nationalistic arguments are enunciated in partial justification of regulation. In the following section the worldwide pattern of landownership restrictions against foreigners is examined in an effort to ascertain whether or not internal rent-seeking behavior can explain regulation on the external margin.

Worldwide Property-Rights Restrictions

In order to put the rent-seeking theory of regulation against foreigners to the test of explaining the worldwide status of nonresident alien tenure of property rights, it is necessary to examine first the pattern of relevant international laws in existence.

Communist countries do not generally permit direct investment by foreigners. All of the land belongs to the state, and ownership rights may not be held by non-nationals. However, most foreign countries, communist or noncommunist, that have an official policy that prohibits foreign direct investment in real estate, permit long-term leases or some similar form of holding an interest in real estate. In such cases, the uses made of such property are limited expressly to purposes spelled out in foreign-investment statutes.[6]

Location of country seems to have some bearing on the nature of a country's treatment of foreign investors in their real estate. Seven of the eleven most permissive countries are located in western Europe. These countries are Belgium, Italy, Luxembourg, the Netherlands, Portugal, the United Kingdom, and West Germany. Most of the countries that permit foreign ownership except along their borders are located in South America, and include Chile, Mexico, Panama, and Peru (see table 7–1). The most restrictive countries are found generally in Asia: Hong Kong, Indonesia, Iran, the Philippines, and Thailand prohibit nonresident alien ownership of land.

Border restrictions typically take the form of prohibitions against foreign ownership of land within a 50-or 100-kilometer strip bordering the country in question. They can be explained in reference to one (or both) of two theories. First, border restrictions may be viewed as a rational response to real or imagined threats to a nation's sovereignty (that is, continued tenure in office by the current head of state). Second, rent-seeking considerations might prevail to such an extent in a country's government that otherwise undesirable border restrictions are enacted. Suppose, for example, that some special-interest group within the affected country lobbies the appropriate authorities for a transfer of wealth (income). It is, as previously mentioned, less costly to steal from outsiders than from insiders in order to keep the interest group happy, yet the government may be reluctant to bar foreigners completely from undertaking investment in the country. The interest group's response is to use nationalism as a vehicle to reach a low-cost compromise; arguing that the well-being (security) of the country is threat-

Table 7–1
Worldwide Legal Restrictions on Foreign Ownership of Real Estate

Category	Country	Region
No restrictions	Belgium	Europe
	West Germany	Europe
	Italy	Europe
	Luxembourg	Europe
	Netherlands	Europe
	Pakistan	Asia
	Portugal	Europe
	Puerto Rico	North America
	United Kingdom	Europe
	Uruguay	South America
	Venezuela	South America
Border restrictions	Chile	South America
	Greece	Europe
	Mexico	South America
	Panama	South America
	Peru	South America
	Sweden	Europe
Minor restrictions	Austria	Europe
	Australia	Australia
	Canada	North America
	Finland	Europe
	France	Europe
	Ghana	Africa
	India	Asia
	Israel	Asia
	Jordan	Asia
	Malaysia	Asia
	Norway	Europe
	Taiwan	Asia
	Turkey	Europe
Special rules	Brazil	South America
	Lebanon	Asia
	Saudi Arabia	Asia
	South Africa	Africa
	Spain	Europe
Major restrictions	Argentina	South America
	Columbia	South America
	Denmark	Europe
	Ireland	Europe
	Japan	Asia
	Korea	Asia
	Singapore	Asia
	Switzerland	Europe
Prohibition of alien ownership	Czechoslovakia	Europe
	Ecuador	South America
	Hong Kong	Asia
	Indonesia	Asia
	Iran	Asia
	Liberia	Africa
	New Zealand	Australia
	Nigeria	Africa
	Philippines	Asia
	Thailand	Asia
	USSR	Europe

Source: Adapted from *Real Estate Review*, vol. 10, no. 1 (Spring 1980), p. 114.

ened in some fashion by the presence of alien landowners. Such arguments may persuade even the most tolerant of governments into enactment of border restrictions against foreigners.

There is a very real difference between these two theories. In the context of the first theory, the government itself is motivated to institute restrictions against foreigners. Such restrictions are motivated by hopes of a favorable income redistribution in the latter case, as the group seeking favorable wealth redistributions petitions the government to act in its behalf.

Almost all foreign countries specifically exclude foreign investment in particular economic sectors or types of business. The form of these restrictions differs widely. In some cases, restrictions may prohibit any use of real estate other than that for which approval has been granted. In other cases, foreigners are only able to hold a minority interest in property located in a restricted sector. In the event that a sector is considered sensitive, foreign-investment legislation may require only that approval be obtained from the appropriate official before claiming ownership status.

It should come as no surprise then that various minor and major legal restrictions and special rules appear to differentially benefit identifiable subsets of the enacting nations' populations. In Spain, for example, foreigners may not acquire rights of ownership to mines, quarries, or other subsurface extraction industries. The state maintains all rights thereto, and may exploit them directly or contract for their exploitation with Spanish individuals or companies.[7] Foreign capital that is invested in Saudi Arabia is limited in its use to projects for economic development only—investment in activities of a purely commercial nature is not permitted. In Iran, foreign ownership of real estate is permitted for residential use only. Swiss law requires licensing of nonresident aliens who wish to acquire an interest in real estate. However, licenses are given to acquire real estate for investment purposes, only for new, low-rent housing.

In Argentina, foreign investment in eight types of business activity is strictly forbidden. These activities include agriculture, stock breeding, forestry, insurance, commercial banking, and enterprises engaged in media production. In Austria, regulations restrict the right of foreigners to engage in certain trades, businesses, and professions, such as banking, insurance, the tourist trade, and state monopolies. In France, marine, air and land transportation, petroleum extraction, banking, and insurance are withdrawn altogether from foreign investment, although in some cases, an outsider can obtain special authorization to engage in one of these otherwise restricted trades.

With respect to the French example, legal restriction of foreign ownership of real estate has the effect of restricting the degree of competition given nationals by foreign producers. In other instances, restrictions are aimed specifically at provision of jobs for nationals (Breton's theory). In

Saudi Arabia and Iran, the granting of certain benefits is linked to having a minimum amount of local participation. In the Andean Common Regime, sectoral restrictions vary according to the degree of participation by nationals in the investment projects. Similar restrictions exist in Australia, the Dominican Republic, and Japan.[8]

Concluding Comments on Nationalism

In each of the cases presented here, it is not terribly difficult to figure out who are the probable beneficiaries of the restrictive regulations. In Austria, for example, individuals engaged in the banking, insurance, tourism industries, and the state monopolies are automatically immune from competition from outsiders. At the very least, this should have a non-negative effect on profitability. Owners of specialized resources are the beneficiaries of regulation that stems out of fears that foreigners will gain some sort of strategic control over their country's vital resources.

Even though the foregoing survey of international landownership restrictions against foreigners is by no means exhaustive, the evidence available is suggestive. In particular, it suggests that the rent-seeking theory of restrictive regulation cannot be rejected as an explanation for some degree of the variation in the pattern of property-rights restriction that existed throughout the world as of 1979.

Restrictions on Corporate Ownership of U.S. Farmland

It was argued in chapters 4 and 5 that as net demanders of farmland, small, family farmers would prefer to restrict whatever components of the demand for farmland are feasible, on the margin. That is, regulation of domestic demand for farmland would also aid small farmers who face expansion in order to keep up with a steadily increasing minimum-size farm requirement. The costs of regulating against fellow U.S. citizens was passed off, at that time, as being considerably higher than the cost of regulating foreigners.

It was pointed out that although the increment to farmland price inflation contributed by foreign buyers is very small, it is precisely the small changes in price, rather than the large changes, that motivate farmers to seek regulation; and that regulation of foreigners could be obtained at a fairly low cost to small farmers, in terms of lobbying time and expenditures.

The cost of restricting fellow resident U.S. nationals from participation in the market for U.S. farmland is undoubtedly much higher—such restrictions would be declared unconstitutional, no doubt. Despite this fact, farmers in certain states have been successful at restricting a second component of the demand side of the market for U.S. farmland: U.S. corporations. These states are listed in table 7-2. With respect to the degree of participation by corporations in the business of agriculture, arguments for and against regulation, the circumstances surrounding restrictive legislation aimed at preventing corporate participation in agriculture are virtually identical to the ones identified previously with respect to restriction against foreign owners.

The incidence of corporate farming is examined in the next section, followed by a comparison of the success or failure of legislation designed to prohibit corporate participation in the market for U.S. farmland with the success or failure of similar legislation aimed at nonresident aliens. It is found that there is a high, positive correlation between ability to regulate against foreigners and the ability to regulate against U.S. corporations.

The Scope of Corporate Farming

With the exception of large, highly integrated corporations that produce certain crops (nuts, citrus fruits, broilers, (poultry), surgarcane, and sugar beets), the incidence of large, corporate agribusiness is quite low. In 1969,

Table 7-2
States with Restrictions on Corporate Farming

Category	State
Enacted restrictions	Arizona
	Iowa
	Kansas
	Kentucky
	Minnesota
	Mississippi
	Missouri
	Nebraska
	North Dakota
	Oklahoma
	South Dakota
	Texas
	Wisconsin
Proposed restrictions	Colorado
	Illinois
	Indiana
	Oregon
	Tennessee
	West Virginia

Source: USDA, *Monitoring Foreign Ownership of U.S. Real Estate* Report to Congress (1979); USDA, Economic Research Service *State Laws Relating to the Ownership of U.S. Land by Aliens and Business Entities* (November 1981).

for example, total agricultural production by widely held corporations (ten or more shareholders) was only 3 percent of total U.S. production; in 1974 the figure had risen, but only to 5 percent. Proprietorships and family corporations (fewer than ten shareholders) comprised 99 percent of all farms and accounted for 95 percent of all farm sales in 1974.[9] Evidence presented in chapter 3 suggests that a large percentage of the increase in price of agricultural lands during the 1960s and 1970s can be explained by bidding among existing farmers.

The degree of landownership by widely held corporations is of approximately the same order of magnitude as that held by foreigners. In the corn belt, corporate farmland accounted for less than 3 percent of the land area in farms in 1974, and widely held corporations owned only a small part of that.

If the theory proposed in chapter 3 is correct, small increments to agricultural land-price inflation of the kind induced by corporate farming may serve to lower the net value of small, family farmers' (human plus nonhuman) capital. On the other hand, a corporate presence in the agricultural sector that contributed significantly to a rapid rate of land-price increase would be welcomed by farmers, since the rise in the capital value of their landholdings would overwhelm negative effects on the value of their human capital.

Large corporate ventures in agriculture have never enjoyed much success in the United States, save with respect to a few, selected commodities. The apparent reason for this lack of success involves diseconomies of management. On a large farm it is exceptionally difficult to monitor productivity of hired laborers, and shirking is not uncommon. The historical remedy to this problem is decentralization of property rights in farming. As a result of the small-farm structure in U.S. agriculture, restrictions, against corporate farming are seldom opposed in the state legislatures. The usual exception to this rule is the case in which one of the larger operations is physically located within the state contemplating regulation. In the few states that do support a relatively high percentage of widely held corporations in agriculture, restrictions against corporate ownership of farmland or corporate farming are nonexistent.

This is not a chicken-and-egg problem, either. The attempt to restrict corporations vis-a-vis agriculture blossomed in the 1970s, well after the large corporations settled in their respective states. In Hawaii, a few large corporations produce high-value crops like pineapple and sugarcane. In California, corporations are heavily involved in the production of fruits, vegetables, poultry, feed cattle, and wine. Sugarcane production is a corporate activity in Louisiana and Florida; and corporate enterprises operate large-scale cattle feeding facilities in Texas. Such investment is worth fighting, via the same legislative process used by the net demanders of regulation, to keep intact, and anticorporate farming laws are conspicuously absent in these states.

Predicting the Success of Regulatory Efforts

By and large, it is the states located in the so-called farm belt that have enacted restrictions against corporate ownership of U.S. farmland. A large majority of the states in which such legislation has been proposed as well as enacted (Colorado, Illinois, Indiana, Kentucky, Oregon, Tennessee, and West Virginia) have both a high percentage of state income generated through the agricultural sector, and a relatively high percentage of farmers in the state population. This squares nicely with the empirical results of chapter 5. Moreover, as was the case with restrictions against foreign ownership of U.S. farmland, the national farmers' organizations are the prime movers behind the push for regulation of corporate ownership of agricultural real estate.

It is difficult to pinpoint why legislation restricting corporate farming failed to pass in the legislatures of the seven states listed previously. The simplest explanation is that the proponents did not have the requisite number of votes among the legislators. The not-so-simple explanation involves careful consideration of the explanatory variables utilized in equation 5.1. The small sample size (nineteen states) renders a rigorous empirical test impossible. However, it may be informative to go back and examine the success or failure of antiforeigner legislation in the aforementioned seven states, as well as in the states with standing restrictions against corporate farming, in an effort to predict the likelihood of anticorporate regulation. The results of this examination are listed in table 7–3.

With only two exceptions, all of the states with anti-corporate farming laws on the books have also mandated restrictions against foreigners—a strong indication that the farming interests in those states have firm control of the votes in the state legislature. On the other hand, also with only two exceptions, none of the states in which restrictions on corporate farming have been proposed unsuccessfully have enacted similar restrictions against foreigners, even though foreigners are probably less costly to legislate against.

About all that can be said with respect to this kind of test is that it is suggestive. It appears that the presence or absence of regulation of foreign ownership of U.S. agricultural land may serve as a useful indicator or predictor of the incidence of similar regulation against corporations.

Given the similarity of circumstances and impact of corporate and foreign buyers in the market for U.S. farmland, this association between regulation of foreigners and regulation of corporations, tenuous though it

Table 7-3

A Comparison of Laws Restricting Foreign and Corporate Ownership of U.S. Agricultural Land, by State

Laws against Foreign Ownership	Laws against Corporate Ownership	Proposed laws against Corporate Ownership
Arkansas	Arizona	Colorado
California	Iowa	Illinois
Connecticut	Kansas	Indiana
Florida	Kentucky	Oregon
Georgia	Minnesota	Tennessee
Hawaii	Mississippi	West Virginia
Idaho	Missouri	
Illinois	Nebraska	
Indiana	North Dakota	
Iowa	Oklahoma	
Kansas	South Dakota	
Kentucky	Texas	
Maryland	Wisconsin	
Minnesota		
Mississippi		
Missouri		
Montana		
Nebraska		
Nevada		
New Jersey		
North Carolina		
North Dakota		
Oklahoma		
Oregon		
Pennsylvania		
South Carolina		
South Dakota		
Virginia		
Wisconsin		
Wyoming		

Source: USDA, Economic Research Service *State Laws Relating to the Ownership of U.S. Land by Aliens and Business Entities* (November 1981).

may be, is not unexpected. The rational farmer will lobby for protective legislation on all external margins until expected gains are equalized across the board.

Notes

1. James M. Buchanan and Gordon Tullock, *The Calculus of Consent* (Ann Arbor: University of Michigan Press, 1962).
2. Albert Breton, "The Economics of Nationalism," *Journal of Political Economy*, Vol LXXII, No. 4 (August 1964), pp. 376-86.

3. Ibid., p. 377.

4. Ibid., p. 378.

5.Robert E. McCormick and Robert D. Tollison, "Exporting Economic Regulation," Working Paper, Virginia Polytechnic Institute and State University (1981).

6. USDA *Monitoring Foreign Investment of U.S. Real Estate*, Report to Congress, Vol. 1, (1979), p. 121.

7. Much of the information regarding the specific content of international laws is taken from *Monitoring Foreign Investment of U.S. Real Estate* (ibid., chapter 4). Emphasis added.

8. For further information on this subject consult Bruce Zagaris, "Foreign Country Regulations and Activities," in USDA, *Monitoring Foreign Investment of U.S. Real Estate*, Report to Congress, Vol. 1, (1979).

9. Stuart R. Singer and Stanley Weiss, *Foreign Investment in the United States*, Practicing Law Institute, Course Handbook Series No. 297 (1979).

8

A Final Word

Foreign ownership of U.S. agricultural land emerged in the mid-1970s as a burning political issue, at the state level, in the United States. Although the relative magnitude of foreign landownership and foreign participation in the U.S. farmland real estate market has been repeatedly documented as being of a very small order, the perceived problem of foreign ownership, in terms of farmer response, has been large.

Typical reaction to widespread state regulation of foreign ownership of U.S. farmland at the national level has been to characterize the statutory restrictions enacted by the states as an overresponse to a nonproblem. This is, of course, an unsatisfactory characterization for a glaringly simple reason: if foreign investment is indeed a nonproblem, why have over half of the states instituted legal restrictions against it? Who do you trust to tell the truth—professional researchers who may be removed from farmland realities, or the farmers who are tramping the legislative corridors in their respective state capitals?

In this book, I explicitly put my faith in the latter group. That they have gone to the necessary lengths to achieve statutory regulation of foreign investors indicates that family farmers do find a serious objection to the presence of foreign owners of U.S. farmland. It is up to the conscientious researcher to uncover where the demand for regulation is born, not to question its existence.

The first three chapters of this book are designed to provide a context within which family farmers' demand for regulation can be examined. In chapter 4 it is argued that the push for regulation emerges as a rational response, *on the margin*, of small farmers to changes in the structure of U.S. agriculture—changes that are, by the way, still exerting a pressure on the world of the farmer. The fact that the issue is emotionally charged is not proof positive that farmers are acting irrationally when they seek regulation against foreign ownership of domestic farmland. To the contrary, it suggests that they (farmers) have found a low-cost way of arousing support for their position.

Family farmers have a strong interest in keeping foreigners out of the domestic farmland market; large farmers, real estate agents, and other interested parties have a vested interest in allowing foreigners in. What is commonly depicted as irrational behavior by small farmers (that is, regulation of foreigners), is revealed in chapter 5 to be a fairly characteristic example of rent-seeking behavior, as small farmers attempt to redistribute wealth in their favor, away from interest groups who benefit from foreign participation in the U.S. farmland market. The incidence of state regulation is indicative of the winning group in this struggle for relative wealth determination. In terms of numbers, family farmers have a great deal of political power in the midwestern farming states. It is these states (by and large) that have placed restrictions on nonresident alien ownership of domestic farmland, and also on corporate farming and corporate ownership of agricultural land.

The arguments presented in this book represent a minor milestone in the advancement of public-choice theory. To my knowledge, there has been no previous attempt to apply public-choice theory to the field of agricultural economics. In so doing, we have discovered that farmers are acting in a rational, self-interested fashion when they seek to exclude foreigners and corporations from ownership of U.S. farmland.

This leads to the suspicion that further mixing of the two disciplines may prove fruitful indeed. Public-choice theorists have demonstrated repeatedly during the past twenty years or so (from 1962 onward) that the policy conclusions derivable from standard macroeconomics and microeconomics differ substantially under the normative and positive theories of political activity. There can be little doubt that the same is true with respect to agricultural economic policy recommendations.

Bibliography

Books

Bidwell, P.W., and Falconer, J.I. *History of Agriculture in the Northern United States 1620–1860* (New York: Peter Smith, 1941).

Blau, P.M., and Duncan, O.D. *The American Occupational Structure* (New York: John Wiley and Sons, 1967).

Buchanan, J.M., and Tullock, G. *The Calculus of Consent* (Ann Arbor: University of Michigan Press, 1962).

Edmonson, T.D., and Krause, K.R. *State Regulation of Corporate Farming*. Agricultural Economic Report no. 419, USDA (December 1978).

Fite, G.C. *The Farmers' Frontier 1865–1900* (Chicago: Holt, Rinehart and Winston, 1966).

Gates, P.W. *Frontier Landlords and Pioneer Tenants* (Itahaca: Cornell University Press, 1945).

————. *Landlords and Tenants on the Prairie Frontier* (Ithaca: Cornell University Press, 1973).

Guither, H.D. *The Food Lobbyists* (Lexington, Mass.: D.C. Heath and Company, 1980).

Hewes, L. *The Suitcase Farming Frontier* (Lincoln: University of Nebraska Press, 1973).

Mayer, J.W. *State Laws Relating to the Ownership of U.S. Land by Aliens and Business Entities*. USDA Economic Research Service Staff Report AGES811113 (November 1981).

Morrison, F.L., and Krause, K.R. *State and Federal Legal Regulation of Alien and Corporate Land Ownership and Farm Operation*. Agricultural Economic Report no. 284, USDA (1977).

Paulson, M.C. *The Great Land Hustle* (Chicago: Henry Regnery Company, 1972).

Ricardo, D. *The Principles of Political Economy and Taxation* (New York: Dutton Press, 1976).

Robinson, W.W. *Land in California* (Berkeley: University of California Press, 1948).

Sakolski, A.M. *The Great American Land Bubble* (New York: Harper and Brothers, 1932).

Singer, S.R., and Weiss, S. *Foreign Investment in the United States*. Practicing Law Institute, Course Handbook Series No. 297 (1979).

Socolofsky, H.E. *Landlord William Scully* (Lawrence: The Regents Press of Kansas, 1979).

Wilkens, M. *Foreign Enterprise in Florida* (Gainesville: University Presses of Florida, 1979).

Foreign Investment in the U.S.: Policy, Problems and Obstacles (New York: The Conference Board, 1974).

Articles

The Appraisal Journal, vol. XLVI, no. 2 (April 1978).

Atkinson, J.H., and Jones, B.F. "Should Foreigners Own Our Land?" *Foreign Investment in United States Agricultural Land*. Committee on Agriculture, Nutrition and Forestry, 95th Congress, 2nd Session (January 1979).

Barkley, P.W., and Rogers, L.F. "Problems Associated with Foreign Ownership of U.S. Farmland." *Foreign Investment in United States Agricultural Land*. Committee on Agriculture, Nutrition and Forestry, 95th Congress, 2nd Session (January 1979).

Breton, A. "The Economics of Nationalism." *Journal of Political Economy*, vol. LXXII, no. 4 (August 1964).

Bullock, J.B., Nienwondt, W.L., and Pasour, E.C. Jr. "Land Values and Allotment Rents." *American Journal of Agricultural Economics*, vol. LIX (1977).

Coffey, J.D. "The Future of the Family Farm," Virginia Cooperative Extension Service, Publication 883 (November 1980).

Currie, C., Bochlje, M., Harl, N., and Harris, D. "Foreign Investment in Iowa Farmland," *Foreign Investment in U.S. Real Estate*. USDA Economic Research Service (1976).

Dovring, F. "Economic Impact of Foreign Investment in Real Estate." In *Foreign Investment in U.S. Real Estate*. USDA , Economic Research Service (1976).

Duffield, J., Boehlje, M., and Hickman, R. "Impacts of Foreign and Absentee Investment in U.S. Farmland on U.S. Farms and Rural Communities." Iowa State University, CARD Report No. 114 (January 1983).

Farmline (April 1981).

Farmline (June 1980).

Feldstein, M. "Inflation, Tax Rules, and the Prices of Land and Gold." *Journal of Public Economics*, vol. XIV (1980).

———— . "Inflation, Portfolio Choice, and the Prices of Land and Corporate Stock," *American Journal of Agricultural Economics*, vol. LXII, no. 5 (December 1980).

Fletcher, W. and Cook, K. "Foreign Investment in U.S. Farmland: An Overview." In *Foreign Investment in United States Agricultural Land*, Committee on Agriculture, Nutrition and Forestry, 95th Congress, 2nd Session (January 1979).

Friedman, J.P. "The Real Estate Industry and the Foreign Investor." In *Monitoring Foreign Investment in U.S. Real Estate*, vol. 1, USDA (1979).

Goffney, M. "Foreign Investment in Hawaiian Real Estate." *Foreign Investment in U.S. Real Estate*. USDA Economic Research Service (1976).

_____ . "Social and Economic Impacts of Foreign Investment in United States Land." *National Resources Journal*, vol. XVII (July 1977).

Heineman, G.W. "Pursuing the Foreign Investor." *Real Estate Review*, vol. X, no. 2 (Summer 1980).

Jansma, J.D., Goode, F., Gertel, K., and Small, P. "Implications of ForeignOwnership of U.S. Farmland on Farms and Rural Communities." Pennsylvania State University, Bulletin 832 (January 1981).

Laband, D.N. "Foreign Ownership of U.S. Farmland: The Politics of Regulation." Virginia Cooperative Extension Service, No. 61 (July 1982).

Laband, D.N., and Lentz, B.F. "Like Father, Like Son: Toward an Economic Theory of Occupational Following." *Southern Economic Journal*, vol. L, no. 2 (October 1983).

_____ . "Occupational Inheritance in Agriculture." *American Journal of Agricultural Economics*, vol. LXV, no. 2 (May 1983).

Lassey, W.R., Carlson, J.E., and Dillman, D.A. "The Farmer, Absentee Landowners, and Erosion: Factors Influencing the Use of Control Practices." Rural Sociology Society (August 1978).

Lehman, R. "Foreign Investment in California Farmland." Informational Packet to California State Legislature (1980).

Loveman, B. "Political Implications of Foreign Investment in Land in the United States." *Foreign Investment in U.S. Real Estate*. USDA, Economic Research Service (1976).

Lu, Y. "Technological Change and Structure." *Structure Issues in American Agriculture*. USDA, Bulletin no. 438 (May 1979).

Maier, F., Hendricks, J., and Gibson, W.L. Jr. "The Sale Value of Flue-Cured Tobacco Allotments." Virginia Polytechnic Institute, Agricultural Experiment Research Station, Bulletin 148 (1960).

McCormick, R.E., and Tollison, R.D. "Wealth Transfers in a Representative Society." *Toward a Theory of the Rent-Seeking Society*, edited by J.M. Buchanan, G. Tullock, and R.D. Tollison (College Station: Texas A&M University Press, 1980).

National Association of Realtors. *Membership Reports* (1975–1981).

National Real Estate Investor (March 1981).

New Orleans Morning Advocate (December 8, 1978).

Occupational Profile of State Legislators—1976 (New York: Insurance Information Institute, 1976).

Real Estate Review, vol. X, no. 1 (Spring 1980),

Real Estate Review, vol. X, no. 2 (Summer 1980).

Rodefeld, R.D. "Selected Farm Structural and Structural Type Characteristics: Recent Trends, Causes, Implications, and Research Needs." National Rural Center, Small Farms Workshop, Lincoln, NE. (February 1979).

Schmedemann, I.W. "Foreign Investment in Rural Land of Texas and the Southwest." *Foreign Investment in U.S. Real Estate.* USDA, Economic Research Service (1976).

Small, P. "Analysis of Foreign Investment in U.S. Farmland." *Foreign Investment in United States Agricultural Land.* Committee on Agriculture, Nutrition and Forestry, 95th Congress, 2nd Session (January 1979).

"Foreign Investment in U.S. Real Estate." Report to the Committee on Foreign Investment in U.S. Real Estate and Real Property. *Probate and Trust Journal*, vol. 14:1 (Spring 1979).

Government Documents

Alien Ownership of U.S. Farmlands. Report No. 1 to the Joint Mines, Minerals, and Industrial Development Committee, Wyoming (April 1979).

Nonresident Alien Ownership of Agricultural Lands in Florida. Legislative Staff Report to the Florida State Legislature (February 11, 1980).

U.S., Department of Agriculture. *Foreign Investment in U.S. Real Estate.* Economic Research Service (1976).

_____ . *Foreign Ownership of U.S. Agricultural Land: Through December 31, 1981.* Economic Research Service (1982).

_____ . *Foreign Ownership of U.S. Agricultural Land: Through December 31, 1982.* Economic Research Service (1983).

_____ . *Monitoring Foreign Ownership of U.S. Real Estate*, vol. 1, USDA, Report to Congress (1979).

_____ . *1978 Handbook of Agricultural Charts.* USDA Agricultural Handbook No. 551 (November 1978).

_____ . *State Laws Relating to the Ownership of U.S. Land by Aliens and Business Entities.* Economic Research Service, Staff Report AGES811113, J.W. Mayer (November 1981).

_____ . *Structure Issues of American Agriculture.* Agricultural Economic Report No. 438 (November 1979).

U.S., Department of Commerce, Bureau of the Census. *1969 Census of Agriculture*, vol. 1, pt. 24, sec. 2 (Washington, D.C.: U.S. Government Printing Office, 1972).

———. *1974 Census of Agriculture*, vol. 1, pts. 1–50 (Washington, D.C.: U.S. Government Printing Office, 1972).

———. *1978 Census of Agriculture: Agriculture Census Guide* (1979).

———. *Historical Statistics of the United States, Colonial Times to 1970.* U.S. Dept. of Commerce, Bureau of the Census (Washington, D.C.: U.S. Government Printing Office, 1975).

———. *Statistical Abstract of the United States*, 98th ed. (Washington, D.C.: U.S. Government Printing Office, 1977).

———. *Statistical Abstract of the United States*, 100th ed. (Washington, D.C.: U.S. Government Printing Office, 1979).

U.S., General Accounting Office. *Foreign Ownership of U.S. Farmland— Much Concern, Little Data* June 1978).

Index

About the Author

David N. Laband is currently assistant professor of economics at the University of Maryland Baltimore County. He has written on economics and public policy, as well as on manpower development in the agricultural sector. Published works include contributions to the *American Journal of Agricultural Economics* and the *Southern Economic Journal*.